THE COURAGEOUS KIDS SERIES

Northern KIDS

Linda Goyette

BRINDLE
& GLASS

Library and Archives Canada Cataloguing in Publication
Goyette, Linda, 1955–
Northern kids / Linda Goyette.

ISBN 978-1-897142-49-3

1. Canada, Northern—History—Juvenile literature. 2. Northwest, Canadian— History—Juvenile literature. 3. Children—Canada, Northern—History—Juvenile literature. 4. Children—Northwest, Canadian—History—Juvenile literature. 5. Children—Canada, Northern—Biography—Juvenile literature. 6. Children— Northwest, Canadian—Biography—Juvenile literature. I. Title.

FC3957.G69 2010   j971.9   C2010-903674-3

Editor: Lynne Van Luven
Proofreader: Christine Savage
Cover images: Kid running by Kayley Mackay, Inuksuk illustration by Pete Kohut
Back cover image: Kid silhouettes by Kayley Mackay
Cover design: Pete Kohut

 Canadian Heritage Patrimoine canadien   BRITISH COLUMBIA ARTS COUNCIL   Canada Council for the Arts Conseil des Arts du Canada

Brindle & Glass is pleased to acknowledge the financial support for its publishing program from the Government of Canada through the Canada Book Fund, Canada Council for the Arts, and the Province of British Columbia through the British Columbia Arts Council and the Book Publishing Tax Credit.

Mixed Sources
Cert no. SW-COC-001271
© 1996 FSC

FSC

The interior pages of this book have been printed on 100% post-consumer recycled paper, processed chlorine free, and printed with vegetable-based inks.

Brindle & Glass Publishing
www.brindleandglass.com

1 2 3 4 5 14 13 12 11 10

PRINTED AND BOUND IN CANADA

To the kids I met along the way.

with glowing hearts
we see thee rise
the true north, strong and free

The Stories

For a glossary of words used in *Northern Kids* and more information on this
book and the Courageous Kids series, visit www.courageouskids.ca.

CANADA (Map A)

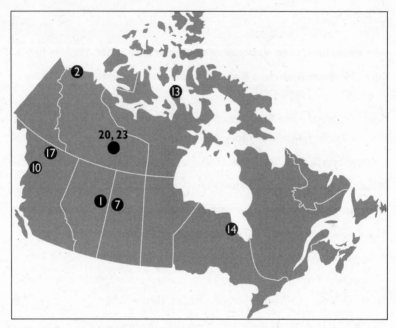

List of Locations for Each Story

YUKON TERRITORY (Map B)

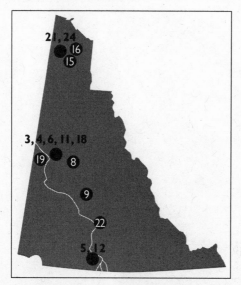

12 **Runaway:** Ronald Johnson, Chooutla Residential School at Carcross (Map B)

13 **Letter to My Mother and Father:** Davidie Pisurayak Kootook, in transit between Taloyoak and Yellowknife (Map A)

14 **The Swimmer:** Xavier Kataquapit, Attawapiskat First Nation (Map A)

15 **Up in My Bunk Bed:** Marla Kaye, Blue Bluff in Van Tat Gwich'in territory (Map B)

16 **Too' Oh Zrii and the Bear:** Tammy Josie, near Driftwood River in Van Tat Gwich'in territory (Map B)

17 **Snoopy:** Erin Browne, Tetsa River (Map A)

18 **Moose Camp:** Breanna Lancaster, Tr'ondëk Hwëch'in camp (Map B)

19 **True North Spirit:** Francis Bouffard, West Dawson (Map B)

20 **The Caribou Hunter:** Devon Allooloo, Yellowknife (Map A)

21 **A Canadian Dog Musher Goes to Russia:** Lexi Joinson, Old Crow (Map B)

22 **Suki:** Laurie Reti and Tianna Reti, Whitehorse (Map B)

23 **Phone Call to Armenia:** Aramayis Mikayelyan, Yellowknife (Map A)

24 **Fourteen of the Greatest Kids in the World:** The Grade 4, 5, 6 class, Chief Zzeh Gittlit School, Old Crow (Map B)

Introduction
A promise to readers

Imagine the top half of Canada as an independent country of kids.

Three immense territories just happen to be the youngest region of Canada. Every third citizen of Nunavut is under the age of fifteen. Every fourth citizen of the Northwest Territories is a kid. Every sixth Yukoner was born after 1995.

If you count children and teenagers in the northern half of each province—from places like Dawson Creek, Fort Chipewyan, La Ronge, Norway House, Moosonee, Chibougamau or Natuashish—you begin to see Canada's north in a new way. This ancient part of our country has been inhabited the longest, its history passed down to us in the rich stories of elders. Now it is the home of the young.

Have you ever heard their life stories? Well, I hadn't, so I decided to search for them.

It was difficult to know where to begin. The Northwest Territories, Yukon, and Nunavut cover more than 3.5 million square kilometres altogether, and yet only 109,831 people live in them. More Canadians live on tiny Prince Edward Island, or in the small city of Kingston, Ontario, than live in all three northern territories put together.

A while ago, I climbed into my old car in Edmonton, Alberta, and drove up the Alaska Highway through the northern mountains of British Columbia and the Yukon. I kept driving until I struck gold in old Dawson City. For an unforgettable winter, I was lucky enough to live in this town on the Yukon River, a place rich enough in kids' stories to delight any prospector. Later I flew up to Old Crow, home of the late Gwich'in writer Edith Josie, and met her granddaughter Tammy Josie, and many other young storytellers. I asked for the help of traditional knowledge specialists in different First Nations, Metis, and Inuit communities. I searched for kids' stories, photographs, and drawings in the northern archives and libraries of Atlin, Dawson City, Whitehorse, Yellowknife, Seattle, and Juneau.

In the spring I travelled east to meet the young people of Attawapiskat First Nation on the James Bay coast, and to search through the collections of Library and Archives Canada in Ottawa. Everywhere I travelled, I talked to northerners of all ages and backgrounds and asked them to tell me a story about something that happened when they were young.

The oldest storyteller I met was ninety. The youngest was seven.

I know I've barely started my story quest. I plan to return to the Yukon this fall because I can't stay away. I'm planning a second book or e-book with more stories and photographs from new places. It takes time to find the far-flung kids of northern Canada. Their country is larger than you can imagine. And yet what a home the north is for kids—and what a home it could be!

Picture a wild, mountainous country with the highest peak in Canada, with thousands of sparkling lakes and an immense boreal forest that covers more than a third of Canada's land. Think of the great Deh Cho—the Dene name for the Mackenzie River—as our Amazon, our Nile, our Mississippi. For centuries Canada's longest river has been our northern highway to the Arctic Ocean, a river with a thousand kids' stories floating out to the sea.

When you're born in the north, you can grow up to see caribou herds, polar bears and grizzlies, wolves and moose. Imagine what it would be like to fall asleep under aurora borealis, the northern lights that bring streaks of magic to the night. You could ride a dogsled or skidoo . . . canoe through tumbling rapids . . . build a wilderness cabin from scratch . . . or kayak through Arctic waters. And then come home to play a video game or a game of basketball.

Does it sound like perfection? It can be, but like everywhere else on earth, Canada's north country is far from perfect.

The wilderness itself is in trouble. Climate change is transforming every corner of our world, but its consequences are severe in northern Canada.

Through the centuries, children and teenagers have endured the North's historic hardships—intense cold, starvation, epidemics and the infinite homesickness of residential school. Life is much easier now, but northern kids continue to experience more than their share of troubles in this new century. Too many are abandoned and abused. Too many are addicted to harmful drugs. Too many quit school, or rarely bother to go to class. Suicide rates among Inuit teenagers are among the highest in the world.

Sometimes tragic stories pour south through a funnel, and the truth gets distorted along the way. Canadians in Vancouver or Montreal or Toronto can watch the news on television and decide that all northern kids sniff glue in the bleak cold.

That's not true, of course. Like all other kids around the world, young northerners have complicated lives that are sometimes happy and hilarious, and sometimes difficult and painful.

3

I went north to find their courage, their sense of humour, their creativity, their adventures and opinions. I witnessed their hardships. I admired their strengths.

Northern kids have shaped the history of Canada, even if their experiences and opinions rarely appear in history books. This is a time-travelling book. Each story will bring you closer to the kids of today. All the named children in this book are real, and their stories are true. Sometimes I use my imagination to create a picture for you when bits of the story are missing.

Here's my promise. Whenever I am uncertain of a fact or event, I will tell you. At the end of each story, you will find a section called *What Do We Know for Sure?* There I'll explain how I found the story, and what happened to the children when they grew up. I will tell you which parts of the story I imagined and which parts I know are true. I'll also suggest ideas for your own northern exploring—on the road, or online. I have placed more information, including a northern kids' timeline and a glossary of northern words, at www.courageouskids.ca and on my own website at www.lindagoyette.ca.

Wherever I roamed in my research for this book, I carried one question with me in the deepest pocket of my parka. Are northern kids any different from southern kids? I think I am beginning to find my answer. Read the stories and decide for yourself.

Is the Canadian north a corner of your imagination? I hope this book will inspire you to explore the north on your own—and to meet its wonderful people.

Linda Goyette
Edmonton, June 2010

The Dream That Saved Me

Antoine Jibeau, age eight
Moose Lake, 1870

Last night I had a dream about my grandfather. He wrapped his arms around me and talked to me. I put my head against his warm chest and listened to his heartbeat and his soft voice.

"Listen to me, grandson. Your suffering is almost over. I'll show you the way to a safe place."

And then in my dream he took a stick and drew a map in the snow beside me. He showed me how to find my way around the lake, over the hill, to the trails that would lead me through the bush to the camp of my relatives.

"The trip will take a long time," he whispered. "You will be cold and hungry on the way. Sometimes you will think you are lost. Keep walking and use the sun to guide you. If you remember what I'm telling you, you'll reach the camp of some good people. They will take care of you."

In the dream, I grabbed his hand. I didn't want to let go.

"I'll stay right beside you, Antoine," my grandfather promised. "You won't see me, but I'll be there. Don't give up. Keep walking."

And then I woke up again.

■ ■ ■

I'll tell you my story as I walk along.

The sickness came in the early fall. First we heard only bad stories about it from the families that visited us. They said it started in the south, but it had moved into their camp too. Omikiwin, they called it. Smallpox. They were trying to get away from it. That's why they rode north on their horses to warn us.

"Many people in every camp are already very sick," one young man said. "You should leave here . . ."

I was playing with my brother, so I didn't hear the rest. Why should we leave? I felt fine. I could hear my brother laughing. He dared me to race him to the edge of the lake. We took off. I didn't think about the sickness again for a long time.

The seven of us were living in a small log cabin that my parents built near the shore of the lake. It's a warm and comfortable place to spend the hardest season. Our family was ready for the winter. We had already gathered berries and medicine plants in the summertime. We'd dried the whitefish. We had plenty of fresh moose meat after the hunt, and dried meat too.

The cold came early this year, not too much snow, but a biting wind that never stopped. The ground froze as solid as rock. As soon as the ice hardened across the lake, my older brother and younger sister became very sick. My mother fed them hot soup and bannock and found willow bark for their medicine. She burned sage. My father sat and talked to them when they couldn't sleep.

One morning I woke up to see my father with his face in his hands. "Oh, we have lost them," he said.

A few days later, my father died too. My mother did what she had to do. She buried my brother and sister in the root cellar, and then she put my father's body in the corner of the cabin.

"We have to leave here, or we'll soon be sick too," she said. She took us to the edge of the woods where we could make a new camp. She had used part of the tipi moosehide to wrap the bodies for burial, so we could only stretch a wide scrap of the hide across the poles as a shelter from the north wind. My mother made a fire to try to keep us warm.

I still don't know how she worked. She was very sick too. The baby cried and cried. My other brother was too sick to help them. I am not too big, but I tried my best. I was the only one left in our family who wasn't sick.

We ate some whitefish and potatoes and went to bed. Just before I fell asleep, I heard my mother speak. "What will happen to my little children?" That was the last time I heard her voice.

My brother woke up and shook my shoulder. "Our mother is gone," he said. "We have to move."

We took whatever we could find to keep ourselves warm. I carried the baby, and my brother made a rough bed for us on the ground a short distance away from the tipi. The baby could barely cry. We were shivering.

"Go back to the camp and get some firewood," my brother told me. I ran back and found a stick that was still burning, and also some dry wood. I took them back to my brother, and we started a fire. Then I ran off again and collected as many dry sticks as I could find. I took them back again to my brother and stacked them where he could reach them in the night. He was very weak. We didn't talk too much. At last I fell asleep.

When I woke up, the fire was almost out. I knew it was morning. My brother told me the baby had died in the night. And then we heard the sound of surprised voices . . .

"What has happened here? Oh, what has happened?"

I looked up to see four men on horseback. I knew each one of them. One was my uncle from the east. They jumped off their horses and ran toward us. I saw tears come to my uncle's eyes as he looked into our winter cabin, then walked over to the rough tipi. He came toward me. He was crying now, tears rolling down his face. He looked at me and shook his head. I had only a piece of canvas around me as a blanket, with a rope around the waist. Nothing else.

The four men fixed up a shelter for us—with wooden poles and hay—and my uncle gently lifted my brother and took him to this shelter. The men buried the baby. Finally they made a big fire for us near the shelter and cooked more whitefish and potatoes for us to eat.

"I will go to get your grandmother and bring her back here to take care of you," my uncle said. "We will be back tomorrow." They rode away. We watched until we couldn't see their horses in the distance anymore.

My brother sent me to the lake to chip a hole in the ice and fetch some water. I stood there for a long time, throwing stones across the ice. *Clink. Clink. Clink.* And then I looked over my shoulder, because I thought I heard my brother calling to me.

I saw black smoke! Running back to my brother, I found that our shelter of hay and poles had burned to the ground. My brother had managed to crawl away from the fire, but our food was gone. Nothing but ashes in the pot. One more time we moved to another place on the ground to make a new camp. All we had was a piece of the old tent to cover us. We huddled together, shivering through the night.

In the morning, I saw that my brother had died.

I was now left all alone, and for the first time I cried.

I lived through that day—I don't even remember it—and then I fell asleep under the piece of tipi. That's when I had my dream about my grandfather. When I woke up, I remembered what he had told me to do. Without looking back, I walked away from my family's camp and into the woods.

I will keep on walking. I won't give up. I can't see my grandfather's face, but I know he's beside me.

What do we know for sure?

At the age of eight, Antoine Jibeau completed his long walk after his family tragedy. He found the camp of some relatives who took care of him. He did not get sick himself, although many people were ill around him. Somehow he survived the devastating smallpox epidemic of 1870 and lived to be an old man.

This is a true story, but I did not write Antoine's exact words because we don't know them.

Later in his life, Antoine told his story to a famous Cree leader named Joseph Francis Dion. The old man described the deaths of his parents, brothers, and sisters; the visit of the four men on horseback, and their promise to help; his dream about his grandfather; and the long walk that saved him when he was a young boy.

The winter log cabin that Antoine describes in this story was at the southeast end of Moose Lake, near the present-day town of Bonnyville in northern Alberta.

Joseph Francis Dion wrote down the old man's story. He believed strongly that important stories should be saved and passed along to the rest of us—so I'd like to tell you a little bit about him.

Dion was a teacher, storyteller, writer, and political leader for many decades for both First Nations and Metis people in Alberta. He was born near Onion Lake on July 2, 1888, just after the Northwest Rebellion. His parents had been with the great Cree leader Big Bear, and so the rebellion of the Cree and Metis made a big impression on the boy when he was growing up. He graduated from a mission school at Onion Lake, got married, and began to raise his family on the Kehewin reserve, where he opened the first school in 1916. In the 1930s, Dion travelled across the West to organize l'Association des Metis d'Alberta et des Territoires du Nord-Ouest, which later evolved into the Metis Nation of Alberta. As a Cree with treaty status, he also helped to organize the Indian Association of Alberta in 1944.

Wherever he travelled, Joseph Francis Dion listened to elders' stories and wrote them down. At the end of his life, he was planning to write a book about the history of the Cree people in western Canada. He published some of his stories in the *Bonnyville Tribune* between 1958 and 1960, but the book wasn't finished when he died in Bonnyville on Dec. 21, 1960. His family placed all of his typed stories in the Glenbow Museum and Archives in Calgary for safekeeping.

Later an Alberta historian named Hugh Dempsey—a great storyteller himself—worked with many people at the Glenbow to publish some of these stories in a book called *My Tribe The Crees*.

That's where I found Antoine's story. You will find the original typed story about the boy in the Joseph Dion collection, File M-331-30, at the Glenbow Archives. I followed the words in this story as closely as I could when I imagined Antoine's experience.

The Cree people used the word *omikiwin* to describe smallpox. The smallpox epidemic of 1870 was a great disaster for the people of western Canada. According to some estimates, the contagious disease killed more than half of the First Nations people who lived in the territory we now call Alberta. Some people were able to get early inoculations at Fort Edmonton, but thousands of people became severely ill. Only a very few children—like Antoine Jibeau—had a natural immunity to the disease. He lived to tell us of his courage.

Night Magic

Nuligak, age five
Kitigaaryuk, 1895–1900

The days are shorter. The sun is a little dot on the horizon. All of the families are gathering in Kitigaaryuk for the magic that comes only in winter.

A blizzard is howling around our *igluryuaq*. The howling wind warns me to stay warm under caribou skins in my own safe place. The old people look at each other with secret smiles. They are planning surprises for us. They won't answer our questions.

"You will have to wait until every bit of light has left the sky, and all of our visitors get here," *anaanak* whispered to me. "Just be patient."

For hours I watched the *katak* with terror and excitement in my stomach. I waited for the mysterious creatures to jump through the entrance just the way they did last winter. At last I heard the first fierce growling . . .

All the children started to shriek at once. An old man, our leader, shouted "Aaa!" Older people began to sing songs, louder and louder, as the growling came closer and closer.

"Grr!"

A huge brown bear came crawling through the entrance into our home! It stood up on its hind legs and reached up to touch the roof with its front paws. I saw the bear's giant shadow on the wall behind me. I saw his sharp claws and his long, pointed teeth. Just as the bear leapt toward me, I jumped under the caribou skins to hide from him.

A few moments later, *anaanak* murmured to me, "He's gone. You can come out now."

My grandmother gave me a bit of dried fish to take away my worries. I huddled closer to her, nibbling my treat and watching the door. Soon I heard fierce growling again, even worse than before. I could hear a big animal's shuffling and bumping against the ice walls, the grunting and roaring, the grinding of big teeth. Old people began to sing again, and then . . .

"Grr!"

This time a huge polar bear crawled through the entrance and into the room!

The hungry animal raced around the circle, searching the faces of people in the lamplight until it found me. The polar bear pounced!

With a shriek, I disappeared under the caribou skins for the second time. I trembled and shivered, waiting to be eaten alive. Then I heard the soft laughter of my grandmother.

"Come out, come out," *anaanak* said to me. "This is no night to sleep."

She pulled me toward her. I fell asleep watching the tug-of-war contest.

The next night, the old man, our leader, stood up and said: "Tonight the *itkrilit* will come. Sing some more." I didn't know this song and it had a difficult tune. While I was listening to the older people singing, I heard something hit the outside walls of our house.

A stranger crawled through the entrance. He wore clothes that didn't look like ours, and his hair was long. When he saw us, he pulled a long wooden knife from his pack.

"You have nothing to fear here; come in," our leader told the stranger. "Where do you come from?"

The mysterious man answered: "I come from far away by a long road. I'm cold. I wish to see Inuit. You are also glad to look me over."

We stared at him as he started to dance. The young stranger was a good dancer and he liked our singing. When the old man told him it was time to go, he leapt to his feet and scattered a shower of toys, beads, and caribou treats behind him as he ran out the door.

I scrambled to pick them up first. My cousins also searched the floor for the gifts. I drifted off to sleep and dreamed of the stranger's country far away.

The next night, our leader called out to each elder by name to send the *tunrait* into our home. Soon new creatures arrived, one after another: foxes of all colours, weasels and ducks, and many new bears. A tall swan hopped through the door, flapped its wings, and bent its long neck before disappearing into the long passage. Then a white fox ran into the room to nibble fish scraps from the corner.

I ate and ate as I watched each creature with a little less fear. I listened to the drumming and songs, and watched games like *orsiktartut*.

Many hours later, drowsy in the lamplight, I fell asleep just as the older men began to throw feathered darts at a target in the middle of the room.

That was the last game of the *kaivitjvik*, our time of dancing and happiness, which begins when the sun goes away and ends when the sun comes back to us.

What do we know for sure?

This story comes from a great storyteller of the Arctic, a man named Nuligak, who described the excitement of *kaivitjvik*—the long winter celebration—in one of his early stories about his childhood.

Nuligak was born in 1895 in the homeland of the Inuvialuit, which translated into English means the "real people." For the past seven hundred years, maybe longer, the Inuvialuit have lived in the northwestern part of our continent around the Beaufort Sea and the Mackenzie Delta in the Northwest Territories.

Nuligak was an orphan who never knew his parents. His grandmother took care of him, although she had a problem with one leg and couldn't walk. They shared many terrible hardships and adventures before her death, and the boy showed his courage whenever he encountered danger and starvation. He grew up to be one of the first Inuvialuit to learn how to read and write.

We know about Nuligak because he wrote his own life story down on paper. He had a friend named Maurice Metayer, an Oblate priest from France who lived with the Inuvialuit and learned to speak their language. The priest translated his friend's words into English and edited the story for a book, *I, Nuligak*, which was published in 1966 when Nuligak was an old man.

"I, Nuligak, will tell you a story," it begins. "It is the story of what has happened to me in my life, all my adventures . . ."

Nuligak's family travelled widely across the land on their hunting trips, but they made their seasonal camps at Kitigaaryuk, a traditional village near the mouth of the Mackenzie Delta, not too far from present-day Tuktoyaktuk.

When Nuligak was a young boy, as many as one thousand Kitigaaryungmiut would gather near the village every summer to hunt beluga whales in *qayaqs*, the small boats we know as kayaks. After hunting trips on the land, they returned to the village to live together through the coldest and hardest part of the winter.

The families carved igloos from snow as temporary shelters when they were hunting on the land, but in the village they made larger homes called *igluryuaq*. These houses were shaped like the snow igloos, but made out of driftwood and earth. Covered with layers of snow and ice, these houses were big enough inside to be a home to several families. People sat and slept on platforms in a circle. The only window was a hole in the roof that could be covered in severe weather. The door, or *katak*, opened to a narrow passageway to the outside.

The Inuvialuit live in one of the coldest places on Earth, a place with no daylight at all through thirty days in the deepest part of winter.

More than a century ago, when Nuligak was little, families had no stove or fire, but they were warm. Carved stone lamps called *kudlik* or *qulliq* were filled with animal oil and small wicks. They burned all the time to provide both light and heat.

All through the long winter, the Inuvialuit told stories and organized long winter entertainments for themselves.

I retold a part of Nuligak's story about his childhood memories of the *kaivitjvik*, from his point of view as a five-year-old. In his book, he described the way adults would stuff the skins of brown bears and polar bears and enter the house wearing them as a costume over their backs. The bears looked so real that young children would be frightened of them—for a while.

Other people would dress up as the *itkrilit*—their own word for the First Nations people who were often their enemy in ancient wars. However, in these visits the pretend strangers would leave treats and toys for the children.

Other entertainment included wrestling matches, dart games, and games of strength. In one game, *orsiktartut*, two ropes were attached to the roof of the house. Someone sitting on the floor would grab the ends of the ropes to lift himself up from the floor and back down. In another jumping game, people would try to touch the roof of the house with their toe.

Working at night to hide their crafts from children, the elders would prepare beautiful and lifelike puppets of legendary figures called *tunrait* or *tunraq*. These figures would come into the house, one by one, to tell stories to the people. Once again, the smallest children would believe they were real animals.

Nuligak said he never learned how to make the puppets himself. "Before we youngsters could learn from the old, a severe illness carried them away. They were so wary of giving away their secret that it died with them."

In 1932, after a series of severe epidemics and hardship, many people of Kitigaaryuk moved to Tuktoyaktuk. Over time, the community disappeared, but the special place is still visited by the Inuvialuit and other northern travellers.

The Inuvialuit of the Northwest Territories are related to the Inuit in other parts of Canada—in Nunavut territory, in the Nunavik region in the northern third of Quebec, and in the Nunatsiavut area on the coast of Labrador.

Altogether about forty-five thousand Inuit live in Canada, and most live in the Arctic. They are related to the Inupiat in

Alaska, to the Yuit in Alaska and eastern Russia, and to the Inuit in Greenland. While the word Eskimo is still used in Alaska and elsewhere in the United States, it is no longer used in Canada.

The Inuit speak many dialects—not just one—and people in each region have their own history, traditions, and dialects.

The Inuvialuit speak a dialect called Inuvialuktun. This was Nuligak's language, and I have used some of the words in this story. For example, *anaanak* means "grandmother" in English.

To see pictures of Nuligak and many other Inuvialuit communities—in the past and in the present—visit www.pwnhc.ca and the wonderful online exhibits of the Prince of Wales Northern Heritage Centre in Yellowknife. One exhibit is just for kids, and it's called Journey to Kitigaaryuk. You can hear people speaking in Inuvialuktun, and see what an *igluryuaq* looked like on the inside when Nuligak lived in one.

Later in his life, Nuligak was sometimes known by his English name, Bob Cockney. He died at the age of seventy-one in an Edmonton hospital in 1966, the same year his book was published. His book is now out of print, but you can ask for it in the library. He tells an unforgettable story.

Chief Isaac and his son, 1899.

The Photograph

A little boy and his father, Chief Isaac
on Tr'ondëk Hwëch'in land, 1899

—Where are we going, Papa?

—I am taking you to town, son

—Will you carry me on your shoulder into town?

—I will carry you high on my shoulder so nobody will bump you.

—Why are we going into town?

—Mr. Duclos is going to make a picture of us.

—Why do we need a picture?

—So that when you are an old man, you will remember what we looked like today.

—How will they make the picture, Papa?

—We will walk inside a small building where Mr. Duclos will have a camera.

—What is a camera?

—A camera is a small box that makes pictures when it clicks.

—Will it hurt?

—No, son. Not even a little. But you will have to stand very still.

—Why do I have to stand still?

—So the camera can make a picture. If you move, it won't work.

—But I don't like to stand still.

—I can see that. I watch you running beside the river every day.

—Can you run with me on your shoulder, Papa? Right now?

What do we know for sure?

One day in 1899, a small boy walked into the Larss and Duclos Photo Studio in Dawson City, Yukon, with his father, Chief Isaac.

I like to look at photographs and imagine what was happening in the hour before the camera clicked. The boy looks like he is somewhere between four and seven years old, a time when kids ask many, many questions. I imagined the conversation between the son and his father on the morning before they had their picture taken.

The boy would have spoken to his father in the Hän language. The word *tr'inin* means child. *K'ämänt hozo* means good morning. You say *N'änjit Dähònch'e* when you want to ask, "How are you?"

We don't know for sure the name of the boy in the picture. Chief Isaac and his wife, Eliza, had fourteen children, but only four survived to adulthood.

The couple had two sons named Fred and Charlie, but they might have been born after this photograph was taken.

The original photograph is now in the Alaska State Library. The photographer, Joseph Duclos, was born in Quebec and came to search for gold at Lovat Gulch before he joined Per Edward Larss in a photo studio in Dawson City. You can view an online exhibit of his other pictures at www.virtualmuseum.ca.

Chief Isaac was the leader of the Tr'ondëk Hwëch'in people for a long time. He is still respected today for some important decisions he made.

Before the Klondike gold rush began in 1898, the local people had a seasonal camp in a place called Tro'chëk, where the Yukon River meets the Klondike River. They were related to four other groups of Hän-speaking people who depended on the Yukon River for their way of life.

In fact, the word Klondike is an English word that comes

from the Hän word Tr'ondëk. Tr'o refers to the hammer rocks that people used to secure the salmon weirs in the river. Ndëk means river. Hwëch'in means people.

When thirty thousand strangers from around the world suddenly arrived in their home territory to hunt for gold—all at once—it was a big shock to the original families.

Almost overnight, thousands of people built cabins and dug for gold, wherever they wanted. They camped at Tro'chëk and called the place Klondike City, and sometimes Lousetown. The gold rush brought new jobs and income to First Nations families who supplied the miners with wild meat, fish, and firewood, but it also brought overcrowding, crime, and new diseases to the area. Many First Nations people had no natural immunity to these diseases and died in epidemics, or became seriously ill.

Chief Isaac knew his community was changing very rapidly. He acted quickly. He asked the community's Hän-speaking relatives in Tanacross, Alaska, to learn the Tr'ondëk Hwëch'in traditional songs, stories, and dances so they would always be protected and remembered. He also sent certain ceremonial objects to Tanacross so they would not be lost. These relatives lived in a more isolated place, and they kept the traditions alive for a century.

To live their own way, the Tr'ondëk Hwëch'in moved their camp about five kilometres up the river from the overcrowded Dawson City to a village called Moosehide. They continued to live in their traditional way during the gold rush and after it ended, although their lives were never the same as before.

The First Nations of the Yukon did not sign treaties with the government of Canada in the 1800s and early 1900s. In the

1970s, they decided to reclaim the land that was rightfully their territory because they had never surrendered it. They began to negotiate with Canada for a new agreement about land, resources, and self-government. Under the leadership of Chief Percy Henry, the Tr'ondëk Hwëch'in signed a final agreement with Canada on July 16, 1998, that determined the future of sixty-four thousand square kilometres of their traditional territory.

To read more about the Tr'ondëk Hwëch'in in later years, turn to page 105 for the story "Why Kids Love Moosehide," about a girl named Angie Joseph in 1957.

To learn more about the Tr'ondëk Hwëch'in today, and to see pictures online, go to www.trondekheritage.com. As you will see, Chief Isaac's determination is still very much alive in his community more than a century after a photographer took this picture of a little boy and his father.

The Spoiled Princess of the Klondike (as told by the Queen!)

Crystal Brilliant Snow, age fourteen
Little Margie Newman, age nine
Dawson City, Yukon, 1898

I crumpled up the newspaper and threw it across the kitchen.

Marching across the room, I stomped the heel of my high-buttoned boot on the front page of the *Klondike Nugget.*

I picked up the paper—and was just about to rip it up into tiny scraps and spit on them—when my brother Monte grabbed the page from my hand.

"I take it you're a little belligerent this morning, Crystal? A bit fractious and vexated? Has the Princess of the Klondike discombobulated your equilibrium again?"

My big brother is seventeen. He uses ten-dollar words to impress people. Ma tells me to pay no attention to him. She says it is a phase he'll outgrow when he matures. Believe me, I am counting the minutes until Monte becomes a man. I feel like I'm sharing this house with a human dictionary.

With a sly smile on his face, Monte unfolded the crumpled page and began to read out loud. I clapped my hands over my ears. Oh, not again!

PRINCESS PERFORMS

Little nine-year-old Margie Newman is probably the sweetest and as clever a child as has ever been our pleasure to listen to and watch on the stage. She appears sometimes with her brothers,

Little Margie Newman, Princess of the Klondike, and one
of her brothers, advertising their performance in Dawson City.

and they are both clever boys, but there is a natty newness and conscientousness about the girl that has endeared her to the hearts of the men who go so often to see her. Some of her songs have been heard in Dawson before, but the old rounders, to a man, declare that they have never been sung before with such pleasure to the audience, or to the positive improvement of the song. To your health, Margie!

At last my brother finished reading the article. A few juicy curses sprang to my lips, but I swallowed them with a big gulp. I have to get over my fury, but how?

I will try to put my feelings mildly. I will do my very best.

■ ■ ■

Little Margie Newman came to town this year to pick the pockets of the gold miners. Her whole family went on stage, but right away Margie became the star. She reminds every homesick miner in Dawson—and all around this gold-crazy territory—of a little child they left behind. Every week they line up by the hundreds to hear her sing.

Margie is a little mouse with ringlets. She has round, innocent eyes, and long eyelashes that she bats at every old coot in the crowd. The Little Princess doesn't just pull on gold miners' heart strings. She yanks and yanks at their loneliness until gold nuggets fall out of their pockets.

Can she sing? Definitely. She can trill like an ill canary. Can she dance? You bet she can. She can hoof around the stage with both left feet. Clomp, clomp, clomp.

A few nights ago, Pa put on his top hat and black cloak and

went out to watch Little Margie Newman on the stage. Monte and I waited up until midnight to hear his professional opinion of her performance.

Finally, Pa walked through the door.

"How do you assess the Little Princess's potentiality as a dexterous thespian?" Monte asked. "Is she a proficient and effectual vocalist?"

Pa looked at his first-born son and heaved a deep sigh. I asked the same question a different way.

"Can she act, Pa? Can she sing?"

My father sat down, and pulled a Cuban cigar from a silver box on the table. He poured himself a glass of whiskey, then he blew smoke rings to the ceiling.

"Not bad, not bad at all," he said.

My heart sank.

"She sang 'Annie Laurie' in the usual sentimental way," Pa continued. "She was wearing a Scottish costume, with a little tartan kilt and matching sash, and she danced the Highland fling. The Nova Scotia miners in the audience threw gold nuggets at her dancing slippers.

"Then Colonel Day asked her to come and sit beside him at the head table. After a little while he lifted Little Margie so that she could stand on the top of the table. He proposed a toast to her!"

And then, my father stood up and pretended to be Colonel Day, raising his whiskey glass to an invisible princess.

"To little Margie, the Princess of the Yukon, and dearest to the hearts of every man, woman, and child in the Yukon," he exclaimed, with a deep bow.

Pa sat down again, and chuckled. Monte looked sideways at me. In a loud voice, he observed that his esteemed sister looked flummoxed and flabbergasted. I ignored him.

"And did Margie say anything back to him?" I managed to ask.

Pa grinned at me. He stood up again, and tiptoed like a little girl to the centre of the carpet. He made a deep curtsy to me, and then to Monte, and began to speak in high, squeaky voice. "Ladies and Gentlemen, I didn't come to make a speech, but I thank every one of you."

I was speechless. Monte, of course, wasn't. As he climbed the stairs to bed, he urged me not to regurgitate my evening repast. Pa looked at me with a worried glance. "Feeling all right?" he asked. My eyes told him everything.

"Listen, Crystal," he said in a gentle voice. "Little Margie Newman is a good enough entertainer. But you have a genuine gift for song. You have intelligence and wit. You are more than an entertainer, my dear one. You are an artist."

■ ■ ■

Well, I try. With Ma playing the piano, I practise my singing every day. I memorize the lines of some of the longest plays in the musical theatre. At our Opera House in Forty Mile, I played Menie in *Rip Van Winkle* and Pitti Sing in the *Mikado*. I come from a family of professional singers and actors, not circus clowns, and let me be clear: I have standards!

I have performed just as often as Margie Newman on some of the best stages in Dawson City. I'm not one of those so-called actresses who yodel for gold nuggets and free champagne in dance halls like the Tivoli and the Orpheum. I sing in the Palace Grand!

27

It's true the *Klondike Nugget* and the other newspapers don't write about me as often as they write about Margie.

I check the papers every day. I almost choked when I read that Captain Jack put the Little Princess up on his shoulders after pinning a solid gold broach to her dress. He marched her around the theatre and the crowd went wild. Well, good for Captain Jack. He wouldn't know a good singer if a nightingale landed on his head. He wouldn't know the difference between Sarah Bernhardt and Diamond Tooth Gertie.

Talent? I'll tell you about talent. When my brother and I performed at the Opera House in Forty Mile, the miners up in the balcony showered us with silver dollars and five-dollar gold coins. Sometimes they'd even throw twenty-dollar coins on the stage. Monte and I would run for cover backstage, but then we'd scoot out and collect the loot.

"I could do this all night!" Monte would shout to me.

Back then my brother talked like a human being. Back then, I was small like Margie. The miners called me back on stage again and again, throwing candies and gold nuggets, and begging me with tears in their eyes for one more song.

Someday the Little Princess of the Klondike will be fourteen years old like me. And then she'll find out how quickly gold can turn to dust.

What do we know for sure?

Crystal Brilliant Snow and Margie Newman were both child performers in Dawson City, Yukon, at the height of the Klondike gold rush.

I have no idea if they knew one another, or if they envied

28

one another's talents. I also don't know whether Crystal's brother Monte liked big words. I imagined this tale after researching the girls' true life stories, and comparing newspaper coverage of their performances.

I first read about Crystal and Margie in a wonderful book called *Children of the Gold Rush*, by American authors Claire Rudolf and Jane Haigh. When I moved to Dawson City, I began to search for their pictures in the Dawson City Museum and Archives. Both performers are frequently mentioned in other books about the Klondike gold rush. Every short paragraph I read increased my curiosity about them.

The newspaper articles I mentioned in the story come directly from the *Klondike Nugget* of October and November 1898.

Dawson City was a very strange place at that time. In just a few months, it had grown from a tiny northern village to an overflowing city of about thirty thousand people—at the time, the largest town north of San Francisco and west of Winnipeg.

Most of the gold miners were men. Only a few thousand women lived in Dawson City, and many of them had no children. In 1899 there were only one hundred and sixty-nine children under the age of fourteen in the noisy, crowded town.

To entertain the gold miners—and also to get a share of their wealth—eager business people opened huge theatres, opera houses, and dance halls. When the Palace Grand opened in 1899, its owner boasted that the building could hold twenty-two hundred people. Singers, actors, and other entertainers rushed to the north to get jobs on the stage.

Many of the gold prospectors were terribly homesick for the young families they'd left behind. They loved child performers, who reminded them of their own children back home. One gold miner wrote a poem about Margie Newman that was printed in the *Klondike Nugget* on May 6, 1899.

We see our own dear children by the magic of your art
And affection's fire is relighted with a fierce and sudden start
And you help us bridge both time and space 'twixt we and those apart,
O Little Margie Newman
God bless you little Margie for you make us better men
God bless you little Margie for you take us home again
To Nona, Otto, Ruth or Bert or darling little Ben—
O Little Margie Newman
And we love you for your own sweet self and for the good you do
To the best that's in our natures we cannot but be true
When we find our hearts a-softening with a love inspired by you.
Oh, Little Margie Newman.

You can see that all this adoration could get to be a bit much for the other kids in town.

In his book, *Klondike*, Pierre Berton described Margie Newman's farewell to Dawson City. As she stood on the deck of the steamboat, waving goodbye, a miner named Frank Conrad tore off his solid-gold watch and gold nugget chain and tossed them to her. She smiled at him. He pulled out fifty dollars, wrapped it around a silver dollar, and threw it to her. She smiled again. Frank wrapped a hundred-dollar bill around another silver dollar, and he threw. Margie left Dawson City a rich little girl.

Crystal Brilliant Snow and her brother Monte at Forty Mile, Yukon, 1894.

The Little Princess of the Klondike came back to Dawson City a few years later with her family. By then, the gold rush was over and most of the miners had left town. Margie's princess days were over. She disappeared after that, and I have not been able to find another trace of her story. I did find two pictures of her in the special collections of the University of Washington Libraries in Seattle, Washington.

And what about Crystal Brilliant Snow? Even though she left northern Canada, I have to admit I love her story best.

I learned all about her in a book called *More than Petticoats: Remarkable Alaska Women,* by Cherry Lyon Jones.

Born in California on May 30, 1884, Crystal grew up in a theatrical home. George and Anna Snow, her parents, performed in gold-mining camps across the western United States. When Crystal was three and her older brother Montgomery was five, the family moved to Juneau, Alaska, with a small troupe of excellent actors.

Loving adventure, Crystal's father decided he wanted to strike it rich in the distant goldfields. Her mother insisted that the family stick together. The couple ignored everybody's advice and took their two young children into the wilderness.

At the age of ten, Crystal climbed the terrible Chilkoot Pass, step by step. All newcomers had to carry enough supplies up and over the steep mountain to last a year in the Yukon. The Snow family carried extra supplies for their theatre. Crystal helped to pull a sled full of costumes, a fold-up organ, and stage makeup. For two weeks, she hiked through deep snow. Once, the family was caught in a blizzard and huddled in a snow cave for four days before they were rescued. Later, Crystal said she and Monte had played "igloo" the whole time and didn't realize they were in danger.

At first, the family searched for gold in Forty Mile, Yukon, and then crossed the Canada-US border to Circle City in Alaska. There, they opened Snow's Opera House, a two-storey log theatre. That's where Crystal and Monte began to sing and act on stage for the miners. The family moved to Dawson City, Yukon, in 1898 and lived in a little cabin on Bonanza Creek. At last, they struck it rich—finding gold on the creek and gold on the stage.

The Snow family returned to the United States in triumph, but they went broke trying to set up a new theatre troupe to go to Hawaii. Crystal would later describe how she pawned her gold nugget necklace to buy boat tickets back to Alaska. At the

Three children operating rocker at a gold mine on
Dominion Creek, Yukon Territory, ca. 1898.

age of sixteen, she finally started Grade 5. (She'd missed a lot of school while on stage.) She graduated from high school at the age of twenty-one, and began to study music. As a professional singer, she made a tour of the goldfield towns—including Dawson City—and was welcomed wherever she went.

Crystal led an entirely interesting life, changing jobs many times over the years. She married an Alaska dentist, Dr. Charles Percival Jenne, and raised three children. She earned her own living as a singer, newspaper reporter, schoolteacher, and postmaster for Juneau. (She refused to let anyone call her a postmistress, because she said, "the position is Postmaster!") She owned and operated the Forget-Me-Not Flower Shop in Juneau too. In her free time, she composed music, published her poetry and other creative writing, and worked hard in many volunteer organizations. She continued to give concerts for charity; in 1923 she sang for US President Warren Harding when he came to Alaska.

In 1934 Crystal became the first woman to run for the Alaska Territorial House of Representatives—something like our provincial legislatures in Canada. She had a catchy political slogan, just perfect for the north: "Whet your axes! Down with taxes!" She lost three elections in a row but finally won in 1940. That year she was the only woman to sit in the Alaska state legislature.

She once wrote a little note to herself that I like a lot: "I have done my bit for Democracy and in the doing, have I not gained a proportion of strength which may some day fill a greater need? Who knows?"

A spirited singer to the end, Crystal Brilliant Snow Jenne died near Juneau, Alaska on June 5, 1968, at the age of eighty-four.

A Gold Nugget of a Day

Graphie Grace Carmack, age eleven
Saayna.aat / Daisy Mason, age nine
and Sha-kuni, their friend
Carcross, Yukon, around 1904

Whenever we hear a train's whistle, we smile at each other.

Whenever we hear the clickety-clack of the White Pass & Yukon train moving through Carcross, we think about the afternoon we tricked the conductor.

Whenever the three of us walk along the railway tracks—arm in arm in arm—we talk about the way we jumped on a train when nobody was looking.

Who had the idea first? We don't remember. It might have been Graphie. It might have been Daisy. It might have been me, Sha-kuni.

It was a sunny day, too hot for school. Sitting under the trees, we started to talk about travelling around the world. Why not? Graphie had already been to California. Maybe the three of us could go away together on a long trip? We could take a ship to India to see the tigers, or go to Africa to see the elephants, or sail to England to see the King. He might like to see us. You never know.

Saayna.aat, also known as Daisy Mason.

Daisy knew quite a lot about travelling. Her father had been to Seattle and San Francisco too. She told us that there was one big problem with our plan.

"If we want to sail on a big ocean ship, we have to walk to Juneau, Alaska, to find one," she said. "That's a long walk in this heat."

She was right. If it was too hot for school, it was also too hot for a long walk to Alaska. We stood up, dusted off our dresses, and walked down the road together. Nobody said a word. We were trying to figure out how we could travel around the world without taking a long walk.

In the distance, a train whistle blew. We looked at each other. Aha! Maybe all three of us had the same idea at the same time. And then one of us—and we don't remember which one—shouted the word.

"Whitehorse!"

We started to run as fast as we could toward the train station. Just as we turned the corner, we bumped into a bunch of my cousins. One boy asked where we were going in such a big hurry.

"Oh, nowhere," Graphie said.

"No place," Daisy said.

"Nowhere and no place," I said.

And then we walked right past those boys—slowly, as if we had all the time in the world—turned another corner, and started to run. We raced into the station just as the big train was chugging toward the platform. Then Daisy asked another one of her smart questions.

"How are we going to travel to Whitehorse if we don't have any money in our pockets for train tickets?"

Oh, no. We hadn't thought of that little problem. Graphie and Daisy said they had enough real gold nuggets in their moose-hide bags back home to pay for a trip on an ocean ship around the whole world and back again.

I knew this was true. "But you don't have those gold nuggets in your pocket right now," I said. "We don't have *anything* in our pockets."

Daisy said we had another problem too. "Even if we had money for a ticket, I don't think they let children travel on trains without parents, or grandparents, or aunts or uncles," she said. "The trains have rules."

What do three girls do when rules are rules? We sat down on a bench and began to whisper. Soon we had a secret plan.

A minute later we sneaked past the long line of men and women waiting to buy train tickets. Nobody noticed us. Walking faster, Graphie led us out the door of the train station and around the corner. We crept along a path with our shoulders against the wall of the station. Kneeling down, we squinted over a big bunch of crates.

On the platform, a skinny man in a blue uniform was taking tickets from each passenger. He would put his hand under each lady passenger's elbow and boost her up three little steps into the train. Then he took her suitcase and put it on a wooden cart.

Graphie pointed to a little wagon covered with suitcases and the open door of the boxcar where the skinny man would have to put the luggage.

When all the passengers had climbed into the train, the skinny man called one last time: "All aboard! Whitehorse train! All aboard!" He turned around to put the last suitcase on the cart. Graphie pointed at the train. "All aboard!" she whispered. "Now!" We scurried like three mice up the three steps and into the passenger car.

"We're in!" I said. "Now what?"

Daisy said we should just claim three seats and sit down. And that's exactly what we did.

The train whistle blew. Slowly the old locomotive lurched out of the station, belching smoke as it headed north. Peering over the seats, we saw the conductor walking in a wobbly back-and-forth way down the aisle, collecting tickets. For one precious minute, he took off his eyeglasses to scratch his nose.

"Bathroom!" Graphie whispered.

We scrambled into the bathroom, hardly breathing, and slid the door shut just as the conductor passed by our hiding place to enter the next passenger car. As quietly as possible, Graphie slid open the bathroom door, and we tiptoed back to our seats.

Other passengers kept their noses behind their newspapers and didn't pay any attention to us. Maybe they thought we were somebody else's children. Every time the conductor appeared, we dodged into the bathroom just before he looked our way. We fooled him every time. For all forty-three miles, we told riddles, looked out the window, dodged in and out of the bathroom, and talked about what we would do if the conductor blew his whistle and pointed at three girls without tickets.

When the train reached Whitehorse, we climbed down the three steps to the platform. Graphie went first, then Daisy, then me. The conductor looked at us, puzzled, his head turned sideways. We strolled past him—arm in arm in arm—right out the front door of the train station.

Saayna.aat with her mother, Daakuxda.éit; her father, Keish, also known as
Skookum Jim; and her cousin Koolseen, also known as Patsy Henderson.

For the next hour, we strolled up and down the streets, looking into the windows of all the stores. Sometimes we went inside
a store to inspect the Yukon's candy supply. Then we turned a
corner, and—

"Young ladies!"

We looked up. Way up. It was a Mountie, the extra-tall kind.

"May I ask where you're going?" he asked.

"Oh, nowhere," Graphie said.

"No place," Daisy said.

"Nowhere and no place," I said.

The Mountie raised his bushy eyebrows. "Your names, please?"

We stared down at the toes of our dusty boots.

"Your names?" he repeated, in a deeper, slower voice.

When Graphie and Daisy told the Mountie their full names, he wouldn't believe them at first. He kept shaking his head. We stared at his twitching mustache. Was he laughing at us?

"Do you mean to tell me, you're the daughters of . . ."

Graphie and Daisy nodded. I stood still on the wooden sidewalk, trying hard to swallow my giggles.

"Come with me, ladies!"

The Mountie marched us down the street like we were his little prisoners. No handcuffs, fortunately. We weren't one bit scared of him. For one thing, he had a bit of his lunch on his mustache. We also noticed that the third button on his tunic was missing. He had a gap between his two front teeth too.

"Don't worry about a thing," Graphie whispered to Daisy and me. "If he puts us in jail, we can easily climb out the window." And so we walked into police headquarters—arm in arm in arm—with our heads held high. We were already planning our great escape.

What do we know for sure?

I imagined this story, but it is based on a train journey that happened.

The three First Nations girls named in the story—Graphie Gracie Carmack; her cousin Saayna.aat, who was better known by her English name, Daisy Mason; and the girl named Sha-kuni—lived in Carcross, Yukon, around 1904.

Daisy and Graphie belonged to one of the most famous families in Yukon history. Their parents discovered the first gold that sparked the world-famous Klondike gold rush. The family's sudden wealth affected their entire lives.

I found many pictures of Daisy and Graphie in the Yukon Archives, and many stories about what happened to them later in their lives. I searched and searched for information about their childhood. Finally I found a small but interesting book called *Skookum Jim: Native and Non-Native Stories and Views About His Life and Times and the Klondike Gold Rush*. At the very end I found this short story:

> Graphie Carmack inherited her father's love of roaming. One sunny day, Graphie, Jim's daughter Daisy and another Tagish girl named Sha-kuni sneaked aboard the White Pass & Yukon train at Carcross and rode the forty-three miles to Whitehorse without being approached by the conductor. A Mountie found the children wandering around town and took them to police headquarters, where they spent the night. In the morning they returned to Carcross on the train.

I took this short paragraph, and imagined what the cousins' trip to Whitehorse might have been like. Then I began to search for factual information about the two girls and what happened to them later in their lives.

Let's start with their famous family.

Daisy's father was Keish, a First Nations man with both Tagish and Tlingit ancestry. As a young man, he had been a packer, carrying miners' supplies from the Alaska coast over the mountains. At the time, "skookum" was a Chinook slang word for "strong." Keish became known as Skookum Jim because of his strength as a packer.

In 1887 Keish and his nephew K̲áa Goox̲ met an American packer named George Washington Carmack. The three men began to work together as packers and gold prospectors in a business partnership.

George Carmack began to live with Keish's sister, Shaaw Tláa, whom he called Kate. On January 11, 1893, their baby Graphie Grace Carmack was born in Fort Selkirk.

In 1895 Keish and his wife Daakuxda.éit had another baby girl they called Saayna.at, but she was later known also by her English name, Daisy. She was born in Tagish.

The next year—in the middle of August 1896—George and Shaaw Tláa and three-year-old Graphie went salmon fishing near the place where the Klondike River meets the Yukon River. Their relatives in Tagish hadn't seen them for a few years, so Skookum Jim and Káa Goox and another nephew named Koolseen came to search for them. The reunited family camped together at Rabbit Creek, where they found gold in the shallow water. They staked the first claims, and in the next five years, they found close to one million dollars worth of gold in the same place. Rabbit Creek became known as Bonanza Creek, and the discovery set off a gold rush that brought thirty thousand gold-seekers from all over the world to the Yukon.

At the age of five, Graphie travelled with her parents to the United States to visit her father's family in California. She stayed with her American aunt for the summer, and then her parents returned to get her. They weren't getting along very well. George Carmack left Shaaw Tláa and Graphie in California and went back to bustling Dawson City, where he married another woman and brought her back to the United States. Although he was a very wealthy man by then, he refused to send a dollar to Graphie or her mother.

Angry and hurt, and without any money, Shaaw Tláa brought Graphie back to the Yukon. Keish built them a cabin at Carcross.

When Graphie was sixteen, and studying at the residential school, her father secretly arranged for her to join him in Seattle, Washington, without her mother's knowledge. This offended her clan very much, and hurt her mother. Shaaw Tláa died in the influenza epidemic of 1920. At seventeen, Graphie married Jacob Saftig and had three children in the US. They later divorced, and she remarried twice. She died in California in 1963, at the age of seventy.

And what about Daisy? When she was nine years old, in 1904, her father, Keish, created a special bank account for her education and living expenses called the Daisy Mason Trust Fund. Keish built a big house for his family in Carcross. As a teenager, Daisy decided she wanted to become a movie star. She took acting classes and screen tests, and she lived for some time in the United States. When her father became ill, Daisy returned to Carcross to take care for him until his death in 1916.

Keish left her a generous allowance in his will. He changed the name of the twenty thousand dollars trust fund to the Skookum Jim Indian Fund, so the money could help First Nations people across the Yukon if Daisy died without any children. In fact, this happened. Daisy moved back to the United States, where she married and divorced several times, but had no children. She died in 1938 at the age of forty-three. According to her wishes, her body was brought back to Carcross, Yukon, so she could be buried among her people. Over time her trust fund helped many young people.

To learn more about the Tagish First Nation today, go to their website, http://www.ctfn.ca.

I like to think that both Graphie and Daisy—and the girl named Sha-kuni—remembered their train adventure as one of the happier days of their lives.

Fire!

Ella Day, age thirteen
Dawson City, Yukon, 1917

No matter how much birch I put in the woodstove, I don't feel warm.

"Can you bring in more wood, Ella?" my mother says from her bed. "Please fill the kindling box. Dr. Culbertson says I can't get out of bed for another week or two."

I don't like to go near the woodstove, or see the crackling flames or smell the smoke, but I force myself to do it. We are staying with Miss Creamer for a few more days until my father can find us a new place to live. I know I need to help her.

"Yes, Mama," I call. I pull on a long wool coat, old boots, and fur mitts. Reaching up to the coat rack, I find a red shawl and wrap it around my head and shoulders as I head to the back door.

I step into the darkness of a Dawson City morning. As soon as I reach the woodpile, I fill my arms with birch and run back inside the house as quickly as I can. I slam the back door to keep the blizzard out. *Keep out the cold. Keep in the warmth.* That's what we do here in Dawson City, but what is a girl supposed to do when she is afraid of fire?

I haven't told Mama or Papa, or or even Miss Creamer, about my fear. I keep my troubles to myself.

■ ■ ■

Just a month ago I was the happiest girl in Dawson City. I didn't care if the wind howled, if the cold pinched my cheeks, or if my toes froze solid in my boots. Christmas was coming! Every day our class practised our two carols for the concert. After school I helped my parents decorate our hardware store with red and green streamers. We put a wreath and Christmas bells on the front door. Whenever a new customer arrived, I heard the merry sound of the holidays coming. Small children pressed their cold, red noses against the window glass, staring at the toys on display. They looked as happy as me. On Saturdays, we baked Christmas cakes and wrapped toffee for our Dawson friends and neighbours—and we waited for the magical night.

At last Christmas Eve came. After supper we walked through deep snow to the church for the concert. It was our usual family parade—with Mama and Papa in the lead; then Fred Jr., who is fourteen; then me, Ella, thirteen; then Joseph, who is ten; Hazel, who is seven; and Clifford, who is five. Papa pulled Mildred behind him in a tiny sleigh. Mama had wrapped her in so many blankets and sheepskins that she looked more like a bundle of wool than a two-year-old girl.

What a night! The huge Christmas tree inside the church twinkled with candlelight. Was I dreaming? I think I counted a thousand tiny flames flickering above the wax candles in the branches. Strings of popcorn and little sacks of candies decorated the tree too. The grown-ups loved our concert, and they sang the carols with us. Then we ate treats. We had a magic lantern show! And gramophone music!

I remember singing "Good King Wenceslas" all the way home, and up the stairs and into my bed.

Good King Wenceslas looked out
On the feast of Stephen

When the snow lay round about
Deep and crisp and even
Brightly shone the moon that night
Though the frost was cruel
When a poor man came in sight
Gath'ring winter fuel

Winter fuel—those birch logs in the woodpile—turned my world upside down five nights later.

It was terribly cold after Christmas. Would you believe the temperature dropped to fifty-six degrees below zero? Well, it did. Down below our house, ice fog drifted low over the Yukon River and crept up every road and alley from Front Street to Eighth Avenue. When the wolves howled up in the bush, we knew why. They were just as cold as us.

"I'll pack extra logs in the stove before we go up to bed," Papa said on the coldest night. "Ella, bring extra blankets for the little ones, and hot water bottles too."

Who knows how long we slept? A few hours later, I heard terror in Mama's voice for the first time in my life.

"Fred, wake up!"

I woke up too, to the sting and stench of smoke.

My father rushed past our beds and down the stairs. My oldest brother, Fred Jr., ran after him. We heard the clattering of an empty water bucket, and then my father's frantic shouts to my mother.

"Fire! I can't get upstairs to help you! I'll go outside! You throw each child down to me from the window! The big ones can jump!"

My little sister, Hazel, and I scrambled out of a tangle of blankets. Smoke filled our throats. We were choking and coughing.

Everyone was in a panic except Mama. She ran to the front window in her long nightgown, carrying Mildred on her hip, and called each of our names in a loud, firm voice.

We followed her voice though the smoke. We walked like blind people, stumbling forward, reaching out to touch the wall to find our way. I squinted over my shoulder and saw orange flames climbing to the top of the stairs. All I remember is Mama's hands, reaching for us, pulling us toward her.

"Take Mildred!" Mama said to me. "Stay back!"

I held my squirming sister in my arms as my mother picked up a chair and bashed it against the upstairs window. *Crack! Crack!* When she hit the window the third time, the glass finally shattered and fell out into the darkness.

Down below in the yard, poor Papa stood in his bare feet in snow up to his knees. Fifty-six below zero, with the December wind howling, and he wore only the long underwear that he wears at bedtime.

"Hurry!" he yelled to my mother. "Don't worry; I'll catch them."

Mama took little Mildred from my arms and tossed her precious daughter out the window into the darkness. Papa shouted back a second later.

"Got her! She's safe!"

Then Mama picked up Clifford and dropped him through the smoke to Papa's strong arms. Then Hazel. Then Joseph.

Flames licked up the wooden house, climbing higher and higher.

"Your turn, Ella," said Mama. "Now be brave."

I closed my eyes, grabbed the edge of my nightgown, and jumped. Tumbling forward from the windowsill, I somersaulted through the darkness like a falling star. When my father caught me, we both fell backwards into the snow. My older brother, Fred Jr., helped me to stand up. Finally my mother—clutching her swollen belly with the baby inside it—jumped to save two more lives.

The rest of that night is a black shadow. I don't remember faces, only voices.

Somehow, we must have limped and crawled and pulled one another through deep snow to our neighbour's house. I heard my father's weak call for help, and his knock on the door. I heard the door open, and Miss Creamer scream.

"Come in, come in!" she said, when she recovered her good sense. Next I heard her voice on the telephone in her front hall. "Shirley," she said to the operator. "There's been a house fire at the Day place! Call the fire boys. And send the doctor up right away. I've got everybody here at my house. They're alive, but just barely."

Next I heard the voices of the three doctors who ran through the door to help us. Dr. Cumberland. Dr. Glancy. Dr. Thompson. "Get bandages! Get morphine!" I heard the soft voices of nurses at the Good Samaritan Hospital. "We're here beside you, Ella. Go back to sleep. Everything is going to be all right."

The nurses were wrong about that.

I can't say anything more right now. I will force myself to open the woodstove, crumple the old newspaper, and light the match.

What do we know for sure?

Fred and Emma Day and their six children did escape a terrible house fire in Dawson City, Yukon, on December 29, 1917.

Unfortunately, this was just the beginning of their hard times. Two days after the fire, ten-year-old Joseph and five-year-old Clifford died of their injuries. Their father, Fred, suffered severe frostbite. Their pregnant mother, Emma, had serious burns.

Sad and discouraged, the Day family decided to leave Dawson City and return to their old home in Oregon. As soon as the ice broke up on the Yukon River in the spring, Emma and her surviving children travelled by steamboat to Whitehorse, then to Alaska, and finally down the west coast of Canada to the United States.

Fred Day, the father, promised to follow his family in a few weeks. He loved the north, and wanted to go on one last moose-hunting trip before leaving. As he was returning to Dawson City in a small boat, a huge steamboat passed him on the river. His little boat turned over in the giant wave, and he drowned.

I heard this story for the first time from a ten-year-old researcher in Dawson City named Breanna Lancaster. She likes historical detective work as much as I do.

I met Breanna in the Dawson City Museum and Archives one day. You probably know that an archives is a treasure house of old photographs, letters, diaries, newspapers, and important documents that tell us about the past. I was looking for photographs of kids during the Klondike gold rush when I heard a young girl and her mother in the next room, talking about a terrible fire.

In my usual snoopy way, I stood up and followed the girl's voice so that I could poke my nose into another kid's business!

I found Breanna searching through old Dawson newspaper stories at the microfilm machine. Her mum was helping her.

"What story are you looking for?" I asked her.

"I'm searching for my great-great aunt and uncle and their kids, who lived here about one hundred years ago," she said. She told me she was in Grade 5 at Robert Service School in Dawson. Each kid in her class had to research a story about Canadian history, and then make a special project for the school's Heritage Fair.

Breanna wanted to tell the story of the fire for her heritage project. She had heard about it from a distant relative named Elly Branch, who visited Dawson City in the summer of 2009.

When I met Breanna, she had only a few days left to search for clues. When the project was finished, she invited me to her house at Dredge Pond outside Dawson City to see it. I sat at the kitchen table with Breanna, her parents, and her brother Caden. Eight years old, he is an excellent cartoonist who has written and illustrated his own funny and happy book called *The Adventures of Marshmallow Man*. The other family member is Diamond, a friendly black Lab.

Breanna brought out her project on a big display board. She showed me a family tree she made to show how she was related to the Day family. She also showed me a copy of the old, old newspaper article she had found, with the headline "Disastrous Fire Burns Day Residence."

"I have to warn you, it's a sad story," she said.

The Day family lived at a time of terrible fires in Dawson City. When winter cold was fierce, people would pack wood into rough woodstoves that were not as safe as they are today. Stovepipes would get too hot, and sometimes the roof would catch fire. Oil lamps or candles started fires too.

Back in the old days, the people of Dawson City built their own small log and wooden houses so close together that a fire could spread quickly. Volunteer firefighters did their best to fight flames with their water pumps and hoses, but they had no modern equipment. You can imagine how hard it was to find enough water to put out a big fire when the Yukon River was frozen solid.

Three huge blazes swept through Dawson City during the Klondike gold rush. In April 1898, the worst fire destroyed one hundred and seventeen buildings, even though thousands of people worked with all their strength to fight the flames. Through the years, many families have lost their homes across the north in the struggle between cold and warmth. Many kids like Ella have had to find a way to be brave at a scary time.

Ella Day left behind no record of her experience in the fire that we know about, so I had to use my imagination to tell the story from her point of view. I relied on Breanna's heritage project and my own research to find accurate facts about the fire.

I like to think that the Day family found happiness again when the mother, Emma, gave birth to a healthy baby, Dorothy, in 1918.

You can read more about Breanna's adventures in the story "Moose Camp" on page 165.

Burning Trees, Cool Water

Theresa Desjarlais, age ten
Big Island Lake, Saskatchewan, 1919

We left our home—my family and our relatives—to go hunting last spring. We travelled a long way into the bush, far away from here. When we found a good place, we stopped to set up our camp, four tents side by side, under the Jack pines beside a big lake. Where were we? I don't know. There were twenty-three of us altogether. We didn't know that a big fire was racing through the bush to hurt us.

The sky began to get dark in the middle of the afternoon. Soon a high wind came into our camp, full of ashes and dust that made us cough.

"A fire is out there somewhere," one woman said. "Maybe we should build a raft and float to the island to stay safe." Our parents talked about this idea, but they decided to wait until morning. Maybe the fire was still far away.

My brothers and sisters and me, we crawled into the tent. We stayed awake for a long time because we were scared, but we finally fell asleep.

"Fire!" My father's shout woke me up.

He grabbed me by my wrist and pulled me out of the tent with the other kids. I heard shouting, screams, babies wailing. With my little sister on her hip, my mother grabbed a blanket and a horsehide robe from the tent and shouted for us to follow her to the lake.

"Hurry!" my father said. I ran barefoot through a world in flames, my feet stinging and burning with every footstep. Balls of fire were falling all around us. The Jack pines looked like torches. I saw the world in a yellow glow.

By the time we reached the water, the air was so hot that I choked on every breath. My father threw the horsehide and blanket into the lake and soaked them both. Then he covered three of us with the wet blanket and threw the soaking horsehide over my mother and little sister.

"Keep the blanket wet!" my father yelled so we could hear him. "Don't come out of the lake." We stood waist deep in the water, in shock, as he ran away to help our relatives. He disappeared into black smoke.

I heard a young woman crying out, "Where is my baby? Where is my baby?" Then I heard my grandfather's voice, telling people not to lose heart. "This is an eclipse of the sun, and soon it will be daylight again," he shouted. A frightened relative said that the lake was on fire too. I turned around to look, and saw that the trees on the little island were in flames. Maybe the orange reflection made it seem like the water was burning too. I couldn't catch my breath. I couldn't swallow.

Chunks of burning wood landed on the blanket. The three of us pulled the blanket down into the water to keep it wet, then pulled it over our heads again. A few minutes later, a man, Osimimas, grabbed the blanket away from us. He was desperate to stay alive. We could do nothing except crawl toward the shore of the lake, trying to keep our shoulders under the cool water.

At last, the wind changed direction. As fast as the forest fire had come to harm us, it left to go somewhere else.

The sun returned to the sky. The heaviest smoke cleared away. I squinted to the place where the four tents had been.

Everything, all our belongings, had disappeared. Yet there was something worse. Some of my relatives had died in the fire before they could reach the lake. Others lay on the ground, badly injured and moaning. My father's burns were very bad. The horsehide over my mother and sister had burned to a crisp. By some miracle, they were alive.

My uncle waded to shore from the deep water where he had stayed through the fire. He was burned too, but not as much as the rest of us. He became our leader, and our best helper.

First he walked into the bush and found a small, swampy area of muskeg that had not been burned. He gathered up damp moss and shaped it into many soft nests, each big enough for a human being. Then he came back to get us. Those who could walk helped the people who couldn't stand. My father was able to hold us by the hand, but I noticed he could barely walk.

Once we found our way to the muskeg, each of us collapsed into a different nest of wet moss. A long, cold night began. We kept drinking water. I didn't hear more moaning. I think people were trying to be brave for each other.

I heard my uncle's voice, talking quietly to my parents.

"Stay strong," he said. "In the morning, I'll walk to get help. I'll bring people who can carry you back home."

A few hours later, my mother woke me up. "Your father is dying," she said. He was trying to speak to us. I heard him say to my mother: "I am leaving three with you. I will take two with me."

I didn't know what he meant.

My father died later that night. He had tried to help us as long as he could, but his burns were too much for him. Before my uncle left on his long walk, he carried my father's body into the

54

muskeg and buried him. Then he said goodbye to us. "I'll be back, I promise," he said. "Take care of each other if you can."

We lay in our moss nests, baking in the daylight, freezing in the darkness, for two days and nights. We scooped water with cupped hands to cool our burns, and to help our thirst, but our pain was bad. We had no food. The stronger ones tried to build a shelter to keep the wind away, because most of our clothes had burned too.

Every time I moved, my burned skin would bleed. In a little while I couldn't stretch out my bent leg.

About the middle of the third day, we heard a man's shout in the bush.

We tried to raise our weak voices, to shout back for help, so he wouldn't pass by us. He heard us! Some men came running. They were from our reserve at Big Island Lake, and they had been hunting in the bush north of us. The fire caught them too, but they escaped with their clothes and their hunting rifles.

"We knew your camp was near here," one man said. "We came to find you. We found four of your horses alive in the muskeg, so we knew you must be close by."

Another man looked down at us. Lying in our nests, we must have looked like wounded birds. "Are you hungry?" he asked. "We will feed you."

The men had moose meat with them. One man went back to the smoking mess of our camp and found a burned-black pot and a spoon. He made a fire, and cooked a soup broth. The men fed it to us. It was our first meal in three days. Then the men built a round shelter from willow branches, and put soft moss on the floor. They carried us inside as gently as they could. I think they saved our lives.

It rained hard that night, but we were safe from the stinging wind. The next day the men went hunting and brought back more meat to feed us.

Finally, about the middle of the fifth day, we heard horses with wagons coming through the bush, and many people talking in worried voices. They brought tents for us, and blankets, and a lot of food and soft clothes. "We're here, Theresa, don't worry," one girl whispered to me. She put a soft rabbit skin under my head.

We couldn't leave for home right away because some of us were too injured.

In a few days, our helpers lifted us into the wagons. We had to travel very slowly because the rough wagons bumped so much over the rocky trails, and every bump meant terrible pain. The horses stopped often so our helpers could give us water.

"Please let me out of this wagon," someone would say. "Please let me walk instead." Hurting badly, some people would get out of the wagon, but they couldn't walk very far. So the horses would stop again, and they would crawl back beside us. With every bump and jolt of the wagon over the trail, I tried as hard as I could not to cry out. My mother stroked my head and told me we would be home soon.

Then my relative, a man named House Fellow, died. We stopped, and the men buried him. Our helpers fed us and kept us warm.

We reached the edge of the burned area and made our third camp at Place of the Rocks. Here, an old man died of his burns. He had managed to walk all the way.

At our fourth camp, a terrible storm stopped us for three days. My little sister and one of my grandmothers died there. We started on our way again and finally met a wagon coming to meet us from Onion Lake. They had heard about our trouble too, and had sent the doctor, the government Indian agent, and our Metis priest, Father Cunningham, to help us.

The doctor tried to put medicine on my mother's back. Watching this, the government agent fainted to the ground. Father Cunningham held my mother's hand and whispered prayers beside me. Then our journey toward home began again. We stopped one more time when my aunt died, but finally we made it home to Big Island Lake.

Here, another older man died of his burns, and then my twelve-year-old brother died too. I began to understand my father's last words to us. He had looked at us on the first night after the fire and seen our injuries. He knew he would take two of his children with him when he died—my little sister and my brother.

But didn't he also say he would leave three of his children with my mother? What did he mean? Only two of us had survived the fire.

And here is the only happy part of my story. One month after the fire, my burned and very tired mother gave birth to a healthy baby girl.

My father was right. He had left my mother with three of us.

When I touch my baby sister's soft cheek, she looks up at me—waiting. She is teaching me how to smile again.

What do we know for sure?

After the forest fire, Theresa Desjarlais grew up on the Big Island Lake reserve in northern Saskatchewan with the surviving members of her family and the baby sister who was born when they got home.

Of the twenty-three people at the hunting camp, only eleven survived the fire. In Theresa's family, her father, brother, and sister died. One of her grandmothers survived with such severe burns that people didn't recognize her, but Theresa later said that "her voice remained beautiful to us who loved her."

On a map, you can find Big Island Lake First Nation northeast of Meadow Lake, Saskatchewan. Onion Lake Cree Nation is about fifty kilometres north of Lloydminster.

After Theresa grew up and got married, she moved to the Elizabeth Metis settlement, near Cold Lake in northern Alberta. She was living as a widow at the settlement when she told the story of her childhood experience in the forest fire to Joseph Francis Dion, who wrote it down so we would know it.

We don't know the exact words she used when she told the story, but I used only the facts that Joseph Dion included in his printed story.

You might remember that Joseph Francis Dion also wrote down the story about Antoine Jibeau, the boy who walked away from the smallpox epidemic in 1870. Turn back to the story "The Dream That Saved Me" if you'd like read more about this famous Cree political leader of First Nations and Metis in northern Alberta, and the way he collected stories.

In May 1919, huge forest fires spread across northeastern Alberta and northwestern Saskatchewan. This happened almost a century ago, so there were no small planes or helicopters to rescue families from their hunting camps or communities. Canada had no well-trained fire crews or water bombers to put out the flames.

There were no emergency workers, ambulances, trucks, or even roads to take injured people to hospitals and shelters.

But, as Theresa explained, the people of Big Island Lake First Nation and their Cree neighbours at Onion Lake reserve worked day and night to rescue and comfort the injured people.

Fires are a natural part of the ecosystem of the boreal forests of northern Canada, Russia, and Alaska. Each summer, wildfires burn an average of two hundred and fifty thousand square kilometres in Canada. As strange as it seems, these fires are necessary to renew the forest and keep it healthy. Canada's policy is to fight forest fires only if the flames put people or their communities in danger.

Every year thousands of Canadians—including many children—are evacuated from their homes because of the threat of a nearby forest fire. Thousands more are put on evacuation alert. That means that families need to pack their belongings, listen to the radio, and be ready to leave home at short notice. In the spring and summer of 2009, for example, Canada had 6,556 wildfires of different sizes. Most fires burned out quickly, but firefighters in the Okanagan Valley of British Columbia had to work hard to put out a fire that forced ten thousand people near Kelowna to evacuate their homes.

Canada is very proud of its well-trained fire crews, northern pilots, and emergency workers who work long, hard hours every summer to keep people safe. Many of these workers live in remote fire camps throughout the fire season. On the ground, they use chainsaws and advanced water pumps to control the blaze. Up in the air, they rappel from helicopters to reach remote fires, or parachute into fire zones from airplanes.

Other experts watch for lightning strikes on computerized monitoring systems, and search for new fires on satellite images. Some workers still climb the fire towers in high-risk areas to watch through binoculars for smoke on the horizon.

Many northern kids grow up recognizing a sign of spring—the sound of helicopters and water bombers flying overhead toward a forest fire.

Not one Canadian civilian has died in a forest fire since 1938. However, thirty-five fire crew workers died between 1986 and 2005 while fighting the fires.

To learn more about forest fires—and what we do about them— go to the website of Natural Resources Canada, www.nrcan.gc.ca.

The Iron Man of the Yukon Had Help

Walter DeWolfe, age fourteen
Halfway House, Yukon, 1920

Every old miner I meet on the trail from Bonanza Creek to Forty Mile lectures me about the Iron Man of the Yukon. As if I'd never heard of him!

I've listened to the same stories a thousand times since Tuesday. As soon as an old miner catches sight of me, he thinks he has to tell me the tale all over again.

Last week Stovepipe Dan from Cheechako Hill came running toward me. He tapped old tobacco from his pipe and cleared his throat. No matter how fast I tried to duck behind the tree, I could tell he was going to grab my elbow and start talking.

"Hey there, Walter! Is that you, boy? That was something, eh?

"No wonder they call him the Iron Man! Crashin' through the ice with his horses and his sleigh! Sinkin' into the freezin' cold water with his horses kickin' him in the back! Climbin' half-froze to the riverbank with his overalls ripped to shreds! Walkin' home to his cabin all injured and with his coat and pants frozen stiff with ice.

"And still he carried the Royal Mail! Nobody has guts like the Iron Man of the Yukon!"

I nodded at him, smiled, and kept walking.

And who did I bump into next? Why, it was Scruffy Pete from Gold Hill. I took a deep breath as the old coot grabbed my arm.

"Hey there, Walter! I knew it was you! Now what do you think about that Iron Man?

Percy DeWolfe packing for his journey.
COURTESY OF YUKON ARCHIVES, CLAUDE AND MARY TIDD FONDS, #7103.

"They say he was travellin' along the shore between Fanning and Forty Mile when his dog team went tumblin' through the ice. He's sinkin' and splashin' and shoutin' to his eight dogs to pull him out of the river. 'Pull, dogs, pull!' he yells. He grabs the edge of his sled in the water, and them dogs pull for all that's in them.

"They save his life! Iron Man crawls up on the riverbank, nearly froze solid. Can't even move his arms and legs. Can't even reach his matches or the knife inside his parka. No living soul around for sixteen miles. So what does he do? He climbs back on that sled and mushes on to Forty Mile! They say his feet were nothin' but blisters. His frozen skin got torn off with his clothes.

"And still the Royal Mail got through! What would we do without that Iron Man!"

Yes sir, I thought to myself. You're right, sir. I sure don't know what we'd do without Iron Man.

I tipped my hat to Scruffy Pete, said goodbye to the old geezer, and kept walking. I was just safely around the bend in the river, and into the bush, when I bumped into Old Clarence from Claim No. 6 up on Eldorado Creek.

Here we go again.

"Hey, Walter? You've got to tell me. Is it true?

"I heard the Iron Man came through from Eagle, Alaska, in a full-out blizzard! Worst one this winter. It was dang near forty-five below zero that night. Snow driftin' in front of him. Behind him. All round him. He can't see an inch in front of his nose in the storm. Can't find no trail. Hears wolves howlin' in the bush. Knows he's lost.

"So then his horses get stuck. So he gets out of his sled with his shovel, and he digs and he digs until their hooves are free again. Too bad you can't put snowshoes on a horse. Anyways, he gets back in his sleigh, and yells 'Giddyup!' and off they go.

"A few miles down the trail, the horses stumble and fall into the snow again. Out he goes with the dang shovel. Diggin' and diggin'. Hears wolves howlin'. A little closer this time. He keeps diggin'. Gets them horses out a second time. 'Giddyup!' His team is dang tired. Them horses are draggin' a double-ended sleigh and a loaded toboggan behind that. They keep fallin', and he keeps diggin' them out.

"He gets into Dawson in the pitch dark. The blizzards still a-howlin'. And the Iron Man gets to us again with the Royal Mail!"

Not by himself, he doesn't, I muttered to myself.

I had something to do with it too. So did my brothers and sisters, and so did my mother when she was alive. The Royal Mail couldn't move across this territory without our help. Nobody around here seems to know that.

The Iron Man of the Yukon is my father. His real name is Percy DeWolfe. Sure, I'm proud of him. He can deliver letters and heavy parcels from all over the world to little bush cabins buried under snowdrifts. Those miners' and trappers' families would die of homesickness without their letters from Oregon or Quebec or Ireland or faraway Japan. My dad is their only link to home.

I know that, and I feel good about it. Still, it bothers me that part of the story goes missing every time. The part about us. The part about me.

My dad came out here from Nova Scotia with his pal Pete Anderson during the gold rush. They just about drowned getting down the Pelly River and the Yukon River. When they turned up in Dawson City, they didn't have a cent. Couldn't find gold. Didn't know where to hunt for it. So they set themselves up as fishermen, figuring out that the prospectors had to eat something, and it might as well be king salmon. In the winter, Dad and Pete used teams of horses, and dogsleds, to carry heavy freight for people.

They married two sisters, Annie and Belle Phillips, who grew up here and spoke the Hän language. Annie was my ma.

When I was nine years old, Dad got the contract to carry the mail from Dawson City to Eagle, Alaska. All winter he had to travel two hundred and four miles each week by dogsled or with horses and a sleigh. It was a zig-zag, dangerous route. Dad got paid one hundred and twenty-five dollars for each trip, and that money had to support our family. So everybody at home helped out.

Mama made Dad's parkas, his heavy mitts and gloves, and snowpants. She lined his caribou-hide boots with fur to keep his feet warm. She mended his snowshoes, repaired every rip in his clothes. She washed his shirts and pants outside in a wooden tub, with her frozen knuckles scraping against the metal washboard. She packed huge bundles of food so he could survive in the cold. Dried king salmon. Caribou jerky. Bannock and a packet of tea. And always she put a tin of dry matches in his deepest pocket.

When Dad was away from our cabin at Halfway House—and he was always away, it seems—she took care of all of us.

Sometimes our whole family travelled together with him, babies and all. Ma grew up around here with her people, and she taught my dad a thing or two that he never learned back in school in Nova Scotia. She wasn't one bit afraid of an ice-cold tent in the morning, or a grizzly bear sniffing around the camp, or a pack of hungry sled dogs tangled in their harness. She knew just what to do.

Ma died when I was eleven years old. I am the oldest boy in the family. After me comes Willie. Then Jessie. Then Ellen. Then Bertha. Then Percy Jr.

So who do you think helps the Iron Man of the Yukon now? We do.

I picked up the Dawson City newspaper last September, and it had a story in it about my dad. I still have the clipping in my pocket. The writer said everybody in the territory was depending on the Iron Man of the Yukon to deliver supplies from the last riverboat before freeze-up.

"On the Dawson–Eagle Run, Percy DeWolfe has been busy," the story said. "He's been taking thirty tons of hay, oats, dog feed and groceries and the like down on his boat—the Weasel—and distributing the supplies at Halfway House, Forty Mile, Midway Point and Eagle."

Why didn't that newspaper writer say that my brother Willie and I were right behind Dad, carrying those heavy loads too? We packed supplies until our shoulders were sore and our backs ached. Willie worked so hard, I thought he'd drop. He is only twelve years old! Yet him and me, we kept that boat running all summer. All along the riverbank, we helped Dad build caches and cabins so everything would be ready for his dogsled route this winter.

We chop firewood to heat our cabin at Halfway House while he is away. We take care of those howling, hungry Huskies— summer and winter. We fish and we hunt to feed our brothers and sisters, and to feed the dogs, and to feed ourselves.

We deliver the mail with Dad too, sometimes. When some sourdough miner rushes out of his little shack, half crazed with loneliness, I am the one who unpacks every parcel from the sled to find his love letter from Italy. I am the one who says quietly: "Sorry, Guido. Maybe next time."

Travelling with Dad, we pick up sick people, drunk people, lost people, and found people. We deliver claw-footed bathtubs; axes, picks, and shovels; squeaky accordions; and Christmas cake from jolly old England. When the crowd comes out to meet us in Eagle, all shouting about a dance in their hall, we go jigging to keep them happy, even though we'd rather tumble head-first into our blankets.

That's the part of the story that I want Stovepipe Dan, Scruffy Pete, and Old Clarence to remember.

We wander through blizzards, we fall through ice, just like Dad does.

We collapse dead-tired when we walk through the door at Halfway House, just like him. We never give up.

Thanks to all of us, the Royal Mail gets through.

What do we know for sure?

I first heard about the Iron Man of the Yukon and his kids one winter afternoon in Dawson City. An interesting storyteller named Bonnie Barber came to my house for a visit. As we drank tea, she told me about her father, Walter DeWolfe, who was the oldest son of the famous mail carrier, Percy DeWolfe.

"Delivering the mail was Percy's business, but he had everyone in his family working with him, including his children and his wife," Bonnie said. "Some people don't know that."

That sounded like an interesting story to me. Around the world, kids often work beside their parents, but nobody ever hears about their contributions.

Bonnie told me as much as she knew about the DeWolfe children and their hard work to help carry the mail to the isolated people of the north. Then I went looking for more information and photographs about the DeWolfe family in the Yukon Archives and in a high stack of library books about Yukon history.

To add some humour, I imagined the characters of Stovepipe Dan, Scruffy Pete, and Old Clarence and their encounters with young Walter on the trail, but everything I wrote about the Iron Man and his family really happened.

As usual with other stories in this book, it was much harder to find information and pictures of the children than it was to find about the Iron Man himself. Fortunately, when Walter, his brother Willie, and their sister Bertha became older adults, they talked to newspaper writers and historians about their memories of their father.

In an interview with the well-known Yukon historian Catharine McClellan, Walter said that isolated people along the river depended on each other's kindness, not just to survive, but to enjoy life.

"My brother and I used to fish down at Fort Mile in the early days," Walter remembered. "When we travelled down there, we could not go by this cabin on the Forty Mile River without hearing: "Come in, and have a cup of tea!"

"We just had a cup of tea and piece of pie not five minutes ago!"

"Well, you've got to stop. We've got a big pot of beans going!"

"You just had to stop," Walter said. "That's all there was to it. On the river, the whole bunch, we lived together. When one person got a moose, everybody got a chunk of that . . ."

Bertha remembered that her famous father never talked much about his adventures on the trail, even though everybody else did. "He was very quiet," she said. "He was very proud, though."

Willie DeWolfe told a newspaper reporter that his father once sent him to pick up a very sick man from Lost Chicken Creek. To keep the shivering man warm in the bitter cold, Willie packed him into a dogsled under heavy blankets. He heated foot warmers on a campfire and put them under the man's feet. Willie rode that dogsled for seventeen hours to reach the hospital in Dawson, but the man died on the way.

The DeWolfe children went away to school in Alaska, but lived mostly at home at Halfway House, or at their summer fish camp on the Yukon River. Their father delivered the Royal Mail by dogsled every winter from 1915 until a year before his death in 1951. King George V sent a silver medal to the Iron Man in 1935 for his courageous service to northern Canadians.

Today, the DeWolfe family and their descendants remember the Iron Man every year by sponsoring the Percy DeWolfe Memorial Mail Race along his old mail route from Dawson City, Yukon, to Eagle, Alaska. Sled dog racers carry packets of mail with them, and you can send along a letter if you like. See the website www.thepercy.com for details.

I think King George should have sent a medal to Walter and Willie and the rest of the DeWolfe kids too. Not to mention their mother!

The DeWolfe family had some good advice that the rest of us could use, wherever we live. "Look ahead, and never get stuck."

The Raft Trip

J.J. Van Bibber and Pat Van Bibber
Five of the sixteen Van Bibber children
John James, age eleven; Pat, nine; Kathleen, eight;
Helen, thirteen; and Alex, fourteen
Mica Creek, Yukon Territory, 1931

Getting Ready to Go

We are leaving Mica Creek first thing in the morning. How can we wait a minute longer?

Dad and the older boys finished the last hammering on the raft today. We all helped to build it, and we like the way it turned out.

"Looks pretty sturdy to me," Dad said, with his hands on his hips. "It's no sailing ship, but it should get you to your school alright."

We waded into the creek to see for ourselves. Our raft is twelve logs wide, and about fourteen feet long. Do you think that's big enough to hold five kids and all their belongings? We think it's just right.

Back in the house, Ma repacked our belongings inside the big trunk. All summer she has sewed new clothes for us. She made everything we will need to stay warm next winter: our heavy mitts and beaded slippers, our warmest shirts and heavy pants. She must have checked that trunk a hundred times to see if she forgot anything. Boots? Yes. Parkas? Yes. Long johns? Yes. She packed them all.

We went moose hunting so we would have fresh meat for the trip. Ma filled a crate full of food for us. Inside our grub box,

Five of the Van Bibber children on their raft trip.
Left to right: Alex, Kathleen, J.J. in front, and Pat and Helen behind.
COURTESY OF 2004.5.149, J.J. AND CLARA VAN BIBBER COLLECTION,
TR'ONDEK HWËCH'IN ARCHIVES

she packed bread and butter and dried meat. We'll probably fish along the way too, and this is a good time of year for picking berries. We won't go hungry.

With mosquitoes buzzing around our heads, we carried all our camping gear down to the raft. A tent. Sleeping blankets. A frying pan. A cooking pot. We piled everything together beside the big trunk so we would have enough room to sit on the raft.

"Just remember to listen to Alex, because he's the oldest on this trip," Ma said. "You do what he tells you."

We looked sideways at our big brother Alex. He had a big grin on his face. Would he boss us around like a steamship captain?

"Don't worry, Ma," said Alex. "They can swim. Everything will be fine."

Some people aren't so sure. A few weeks ago we heard a stranger talking to Dad about our trip.

"Now, Ira," the little man said in a worried voice. "Do you really think five youngsters should float on a rough raft all by themselves down the Pelly River, and then down the Yukon River to Dawson City? Why, that's more than hundred miles through wilderness! Many grown men wouldn't do it."

Our dad looked that cheechako straight in the eye and set him straight.

"Well, first off, my children have been on that river plenty of times before," he said. "They're used to it. They've travelled downstream on the big rafts that link together one hundred cords of firewood in sections sixty feet long. They know how to steer a raft, and they know this territory as well as Shorty and I do."

"And second, why should I buy steamboat tickets for five kids when they're smart enough to run their own raft up to Dawson?

"And third, you're not talking about any ordinary kids. You're talking about Van Bibbers!"

The First Day

We scrambled out of our beds before sunrise, jumped into our clothes, and ran to the table as if we didn't have one minute to lose. Time to go!

Ma put a tall stack of hotcakes on each plate. Leaning back in his chair, Pa gave us a tall stack of advice.

"I'm not worried about you on the river," he said. "Just use your heads. But when you get to Dawson, remember this: the white folks in town will say you're half-Indian. The Indian folks will say you're half-white. Stand up for your rights. You're going to be called an Indian all your life. Be proud of that. You're going to be called white too. Live with it.

"Always remember that you're a Van Bibber, one hundred per cent, and that means you were put on this earth to get along with everybody."

Dad looked at our mother as she poured his coffee. "Isn't that right, Shorty?"

Ma nodded. Her full English name is Eliza, and she has a Tlingit name too, but Dad calls her Shorty because she's shorter than five feet tall. When he stands up to his full height and stretches out his arm, she can walk right under it without touching her head on his elbow. She may be short, but we don't argue with her.

Now it was Ma's turn to give us advice.

"Don't push each other off the raft," she said. "Every day on the river, remember that I told you that. If you do it, I'll know."

We nodded.

"And when you get to town, eat good food to stay healthy," she said. "If they give you bad food in Dawson, just go into the bush and hunt or snare rabbits or fish until you bring back good food. You know what to do. Look after each other."

And then we lined up—as we always do—to kiss our parents goodbye.

Alex pushed the raft out into the current, and we climbed aboard. We waved to our older brothers and sister, and we waved to our little brothers and sisters, and we waved to Dad and Ma. "See you in the spring!" we shouted. "We'll be back!" As the raft moved downstream, our big log house on the riverbank began to look smaller and smaller. Soon we couldn't see our family back home—only our family on the raft.

"We're all on our own now," said Helen. Kathleen looked like the happiest eight-year-old in the Yukon Territory.

Alex gave his first order. "Okay, J.J. and Pat, listen. You two paddle, okay? I'll steer from back here."

We hardly needed to paddle on the first day. Our good raft just floated along the Pelly River like a bit of driftwood, bobbing up and down, and taking us with it. We watched little foxes play on the riverbank, and saw a bear pushing her cub toward the woods.

Lying flat on our backs on the raft, we looked up at blue sky. The summer sun shone down on our shoulders all afternoon. "Oh, it's hot today," said Helen, after awhile. "I sure would like a little splash of that cool water on my face. I sure would like a swim."

Each one of us was thinking about the same swim. We could hear Ma's voice, even though we knew she was back at home at Mica Creek, probably rocking our baby brother Dode to sleep right now. "Don't push each other off that raft into the river," she had warned us, over and over. "If you do it, I'll know."

Why do mothers always know what you're going to do— before you do it?

We looked at each other and smiled at our secret.

Nobody pushed anybody off the raft. Instead, we jumped.

The Second Day

We've left the Pelly River behind, and now we're on the Yukon River. Way downstream from Fort Selkirk, we saw old friends on the riverbank.

"Hey, where are you going, Alex?" one kid yelled to us from his family's fish camp on the shore. A crowd of little brothers and sisters ran down to the beach, shouting to us: "Can we come with you? Can we come with you?"

Alex yelled back that we had no room on this crowded raft for a muskrat, let alone another bunch of kids. Laughing at his joke, the kids raced along the riverbank, trying to catch up with our raft as it floated down the river.

Sometimes old people came out of their cabins to holler hello to us too. Each one seemed to know that we were the Van Bibber kids from Mica Creek on our way to Dawson City. How did they guess that?

Alex steered the raft around big rocks and sandbars. "We need to travel about twelve hours each day on the river if we want to get to Dawson before school starts," he said to Helen.

"That's a long time for the younger ones to stay on the raft, but I think we can do it," she answered. "But they're hungry. Let's look for an island, okay?"

It turns out we have two captains on this raft: our oldest brother and our oldest sister. They tell us when to take our hands out of the grub box, where to carry the tent poles, and why we have to take turns with the paddles. "It's your turn now, Pat!" says Helen. "Paddle to that island over there, J.J." says Alex.

We eat when we're hungry. We sleep when we're sleepy. Our only rule is that there are no rules. Whenever we get tired of floating along the river, we pull the raft to shore.

We stopped on a small island to make a campfire and cook up the fish that Helen and Kathleen had caught.

After we ate, we wandered through the trees on the island, searching for treasures. We like to search for old stuff that the gold miners left behind way back in the days when Dad came up here to the Yukon from West Virginia. Do you think those prospectors forgot what their mothers warned them, and pushed each other out of their boats? Is that why all their belongings fell into the river? Or maybe the junk just floated to the island from Japan and Alaska, like bits of driftwood?

On the island, we found—
one old tin lantern
one key
one leather boot with a big hole in the toe
a rusty hammer
one pair of spectacles, no glass
the bow of a fiddle, broken
a rock shaped like a fish
one empty whiskey bottle
an English penny, 1898
a bird's nest with no eggs in it.
"Back to the raft," shouted Alex. "We have to keep going."

The wind howled, and the clouds rolled in. We wondered whether it would rain before we could get to our next camping place.

The Third Day
We paddled all day with the rain clouds following us.

"We have to make good time today," said Alex, steering us around the bend. "Let's go as far as we can without stopping."

When the wind picked up again, Helen opened the trunk and found our sweaters to keep us warmer. Trees in the Yukon turn a golden colour in late August when the wind pulls off their leaves. We saw flashes of red fireweed. As we floated downstream, we watched for bears, digging for grub on the riverbank. We saw a moose walking across an island, with her two calves trotting beside her. A small raven followed us, high overhead, swooping down from the mountains to see how the Van Bibber kids were doing on their raft.

By the early evening, our arms ached from the paddling. Our bodies were sore from sitting still for so long. Even Alex and Helen looked tired.

"If we stop at Coffee Creek, maybe Mrs. Maloy will ask us in to supper at her place," said Helen. "Great idea," said Alex. We watched for the Maloy cabin with every bend and twist of the river.

At last, we saw the little house in the distance. We paddled hard and soon pulled the raft up to the riverbank. Helen and Alex walked ahead of us up a small hill. Daydreaming of sweet cake and hot tea, we followed them.

A tall woman stood in the doorway of the cabin, watching us.

"Well, hello, Mrs. Maloy," Alex said cheerfully. "We're just rafting along to Dawson, and we thought we'd drop by to say hello!"

Mrs. Maloy stared at each one of us. Up and down. Back and forth. You could tell she was counting us in her head. Then she answered Alex in a voice as sour as hard, green soapberries before they get ripe.

"Well, then. You'd be the Van Bibbers. Hello."

Now, this was not exactly the warm welcome that we'd expected. Cold wind nipped the back of our necks, and it started to rain hard. We stood still in the downpour, our shirts soaked, and Helen tried again.

"So, Mrs. Maloy," said Helen. "Is there any place around here where we could camp out of the rain?"

We looked up at the woman, and then we looked into her little house. Just to help her get the hint. She rolled her eyes. "There's a cabin up the hill," she said, pointing into the rain. "You kids can spend the night up there."

We climbed the hill, feeling hopeful. Then we saw the place.

"A cabin! She calls this a cabin!"

It was nothing but a tumbledown shack, an old heap of rotten logs in the bush. We peeked inside the door at the spiders' webs, and sniffed the stink of wet rabbit poop. Rain poured in sheets through the leaking roof. Ghosts wouldn't live in a place this bad. Even the mice and the bats and the rabbits had left.

"Let's just get our bedding in the corner and go to sleep," Helen said, putting her arm around Kathleen. "C'mon boys. We won't let that old lady get us down."

We tried to sleep through a cold, wet, scary night. For the first time on our raft trip, we missed our own warm beds in Mica Creek.

As soon as the sun came up, we ran down the hill to our raft without saying goodbye to Mrs. Maloy. Goodbye, Coffee Creek! We won't hurry back!

The Last Day

Thank goodness, the sun is out again. Our clothes are dry, and we cooked up some fresh fish for ourselves for breakfast.

We rafted a few more hours, and then stopped to see Old Laderoute at Kirkman Creek. He's an old guy with a big white beard that makes him look like Santa Claus. In the clearing, he showed us his ten sheep and the sheepdogs that take care of them. He asked us how Dad and Ma were doing. "Help yourself to tea," he said. "Sweeten it up with that sugar."

We rafted a bit longer and stopped to see Old Cruikshank. Like a lot of old men in the bush, he has no family. He seems happy enough with his old dog and his hunting rifle. He too asked how Dad and Ma were doing. "Help yourself to some soup," he said. "I made a big pot yesterday." We gave him some moose meat when we left. Alex doesn't think his eyesight is good enough for hunting anymore.

We floated on the raft downstream for another few hours, just drifting along and looking at the puffy clouds, and then . . .

"Oh no! Look out, Alex! A steamboat!"

Now, if we were standing on the shore, we'd be happy to see one of these giant boats. They carry interesting cargo, and passengers wave like mad from the deck, as if they'll never see you again.

But we were sitting on a raft, and we didn't want to see a steamboat! If that huge boat sailed past us, it would create a giant wave that would roll in our direction, and tip us over into deep water. Our trunk would tumble overboard with a noisy splash. Our food box would sink to the river bottom. Our tents and camping gear would float away to Alaska. Our raft would smash against the rocks, and split into toothpicks.

And who knows what would happen to us!

"Quick, J.J.! Pat! Paddle hard!"

Alex pulled hard on the steering stick, and turned our raft toward the shore. Helen and Kathleen hurried to tie down our belongings to the logs on the raft.

Squinting into the sun, Alex pointed ahead to a small creek, flowing into the river. "That way!" he shouted. "Paddle that way!"

Alex steered the raft toward the mouth of the creek. The rest of us jumped into the shallow water and pushed with all our might until the raft stopped in a safe little bay under the trees. Each of us held onto a corner of the raft as the giant wave rolled towards us. Up! Down! Up! Down! The wave disappeared. Another one came! We rolled with it again. Hanging on to that raft, we waited until the water became calm again.

The big steamboat sailed away into the distance. We pushed the raft out into the river again for the last part of our journey.

A few hours later, we floated around a bend in the river and saw big houses in the distance. The houses looked bigger and bigger, the closer we drifted toward them. We heard faint voices in the distance, getting louder as we came near.

"There they are! It's the Van Bibbers!"

Shouting and hollering like it was Christmas morning, all of the kids in the town ran down to the dock to meet us.

We'd made it to Dawson City, on a raft, by ourselves, in four days. And do you know something? We always knew we could.

What do we know for sure?

Many Yukoners know about the five Van Bibber kids who rafted from Mica Creek to Dawson more than once in the late 1920s and early 1930s. I wonder why so few other Canadians have heard the story?

After all, everybody knows about Huckleberry Finn, who floated down the Mississippi River on a raft. Huck was an imaginary boy in Mark Twain's famous book. The Van Bibbers were real Canadian kids on a true raft adventure.

The Yukon River is not as long as the Mississippi, but it is the fifth-longest river in North America. It flows from Tagish Lake on the northern border of BC up through the Yukon to Alaska, where it flows into the Bering Sea—covering 3,185 kilometres altogether.

In the 1930s, the Yukon had no paved highways as it does today. In summer, people travelled on the river in steamboats, rowboats, canoes, and rafts. In the winter, the frozen river became an ice road for travellers on dogsleds.

Five of the sixteen Van Bibber children made the trip on a homemade raft in 1931. Of the five children who travelled on their own down the river, Alex, J.J., Pat, and Kathleen are still alive to tell the story.

I asked J.J. if I could visit him in Dawson City to hear more about the raft trip. Now ninety years old, this friendly man has a clear memory of his childhood and his adventurous life as a young man long ago. He is a wonderful storyteller. When he speaks, you listen with your imagination. You feel like you're watching a movie.

Halfway through our conversation, J.J. picked up the phone to check some details with his younger brother, Pat, who lives in Mayo and is eighty-eight years old. Right away, Pat and his wife decided to drive two hundred kilometres on a cold day to visit J.J. So I was lucky to listen to both brothers as they talked about their raft trip together.

Sherry Lafreniere, Pat's granddaughter, also wrote an essay about the 1931 raft trip in 2009 when she was a student at Yukon College. After reading her fine story, I searched in the Yukon Archives and the Whitehorse Library for newspaper stories, magazine articles, and books about Ira and Eliza Van Bibber and their many children. I am also grateful to Georgette McLeod of the Tr'ondëk Hwëch'in First Nation for helping me with photographic research for this story.

The Van Bibber family has a fascinating history.

As a young man, Ira travelled north from West Virginia in the United States to seek his fortune in the Klondike gold rush. He didn't find gold but he liked the wild country around Fort Selkirk, so he stayed. One day in 1907, he tied up his boat and saw a young woman standing on the dock with some friends.

It was Eliza. Not knowing how to say hello in her language, Ira walked up to a young boy and asked him to teach him the right words. Then he worked up his courage and tried to talk to Eliza. He must have said the words in a funny way. She giggled and turned away but soon made friends with the tall American.

Eliza was far from her birthplace too. She was a Tlingit of the Crow clan, born near Aishihik Lake. Her grandfather was Chief Konnun of the Taku Tlingits from around Juneau, Alaska. Her father was a chief too. Her mother decided to take her baby north to begin a new life, and that's where Eliza met Ira.

Ira and Eliza lived together for fifty-eight years. At first, they travelled across the land, hunting and trapping and raising their first children. In 1914 they decided to build a large log home at Mica Creek, not too far from the present-day town of Pelly Crossing. They planted a large garden, and continued hunting, trapping, and guiding newcomers through the mountains.

The Van Bibber family took care of all of its own needs. Far from a hospital or doctor, Eliza gave birth to ten boys and six girls altogether. Two baby boys died shortly after their birth, but the other fourteen children were healthy and happy when they were little. Many have lived long lives.

"All of us children were taught equally," Kathleen told writer Jean Van Bibber in an article published after her mother died in 1983. "The boys learned to bake a batch of bread or cook a meal as well as the girls. The girls got out and chopped wood or ran the trapline. In winter, we trapped at Crooked Creek for lynx, mink, marten, and fox. When spring came, we caught a lot of muskrats and beaver. We were taught to skin and stretch our own furs."

In my conversation with J.J. and Pat Van Bibber, they said that they travelled to Dawson City on the raft to go to school because there was no school near home. During the school year, they stayed in a boarding house for out-of-town children called the St. Paul's Hostel. They often caught free rides on the big rafts that First Nations men used to load with up to one hundred and twenty-five cords of firewood to sell to the steamboats for fuel. That's how they learned how to navigate the river and steer their own raft in 1931.

"Our mother wasn't worried about us," said Pat. "She just figured we knew what we were doing, I suppose.

"When we landed on the sandbar at Dawson, the kids came running to meet us. They had a two-wheel cart, and they loaded up our stuff for us. They were so happy to see us." The Van Bibber kids later broke up the raft and sold the wood for firewood so they'd have a little spending money during the year.

A few years later, the family suffered two tragedies.

Tuberculosis—a devastating disease in the north—came to St. Paul's Hostel. Five students became very ill, and one of them was Helen. The missionaries in charge of the boarding house for children wrote a letter to Ira and Eliza to say they could do nothing to help Helen because she was so sick.

"A Mountie named Cronkite rode his dog team up the Pelly River to tell my parents the news himself," J.J. remembers. "He said, if you want to see your daughter alive, you'd better get up to Dawson."

Worried and also angry about the living conditions at St. Paul's Hostel, the Van Bibbers left immediately. Eliza, Ira, and Ira's visiting brother, Archie, rode three different dog teams through the snow. They picked up all four children who were going to school in Dawson that year, including Helen, and took them home. Helen died at Mica Creek in May. She was fourteen years old.

Three months later, Abe Van Bibber—the oldest son in the family—drowned in Great Bear Lake, where he was trapping. He was twenty-one years old.

The Van Bibber family struggled through their grief. Each of their surviving children grew up to do something important for the Yukon Territory. They made many adventurous trips through northern wilderness, including some very long walks.

In 1940 three of the Van Bibber brothers travelled with their dogs to Eagle, Alaska, then walked hundreds of kilometres along the Peel River to the Porcupine River and stayed there from September to June. In the summer, they made a boat with a wooden frame, covered with five moose skins. J.J., Archie, and Dan drifted down the Porcupine River to Old Crow with eight dogs and one hundred and fifty marten skins packed into the moose-skin boat. They caught eighty beaver along the way. Later they travelled to Fort Yukon, Alaska, and caught the sternwheeler for the long trip back home.

The Van Bibbers greeting friends outside their log home at Mica Creek.

J.J. says that trip was the great adventure of his life.

Two years later, in the middle of the Second World War, Canada became concerned that Japan would invade from the Pacific, perhaps through Alaska or northern BC. In 1942 the Canadian government created a special force of northern soldiers called the Pacific Coast Militia Rangers to patrol the northern wilderness and coastline, and defend the scattered people of northern BC and the Yukon.

J.J. Van Bibber joined the first group of Rangers in Dawson City. By the end of the war, the Pacific Coast Militia Rangers had fifteen thousand volunteers in one hundred and thirty-eight companies, and later became known as the Canadian Rangers.

You can read more about the Junior Canadian Rangers in the story "True North Spirit."

At the age of twenty-five, Alex Van Bibber led the Canol Pipeline Reconnaissance team for forty-two days through the mountains and valleys between Mayo, Yukon, and Fort Norman, Northwest Territories, to map a route for the oil supply line. Other Van Bibber sons served in the Canadian military overseas during the Second World War.

In the 1940s and 1950s, Yukoners began the hard work of building and maintaining highways across the rugged territory. Pat Van Bibber and his brothers Dan and George worked for many years on the road maintenance crews. Theodore Van Bibber—mentioned in the story as the baby with the nickname Dode—overcame severe disabilities to manage the fire lookout tower near Whitehorse for the forestry service.

Three of the Van Bibber daughters—Kathleen, Lucy, and Linch—became well-known artists who painted beautiful pictures of Yukon wilderness and wildlife. The entire family continued to enjoy travelling on the land throughout their lives. Hundreds of descendants of Ira and Eliza Van Bibber live across the north today.

At the end of our conversation, J.J. told me about his father's advice to his children to be proud of their mixed heritage, and to try and get along with everybody. He said he felt lucky to grow up in a large family where kids had freedom and independence.

"We had our own family to play with, live with, and work with," he said. "We were a close family, and always will be. Never hard words between us."

Skeena

Eunice Campbell, age sixteen
Road construction camp on the Skeena River,
Northern British Columbia, 1942

December 1941, Toronto

This is the strangest possible Christmas, for the world, and for me.

Three weeks ago, I walked into the kitchen and found Mum listening to war news on the CBC and cooking supper. I had just finished practicing *Für Elise* on the piano. My little brother, Bill, was reading the funny papers. Dad sat beside him at the kitchen table, twisting tobacco into cigarette papers, and sneaking bits of sausage to Gyp under the table whenever my mother looked the other way.

We are hardly ever in one room together, I thought. And this won't last long.

"Shh! Listen!" Mum turned up the radio dial and we heard the familiar American accent of President Roosevelt in the United States . . .

"Yesterday, December 7, 1941—a date which will live in infamy—the United States of America was suddenly and deliberately attacked by naval and air forces of the Empire of Japan . . ."

My brother Bill is only eleven, but he didn't need Mr. Roosevelt to tell him that the whole world is tangled up in trouble. "That mean the Yanks will go to war too now, right?" My parents nodded. The war is spreading through Europe, Russia, China, and North Africa. We send food parcels to our grandparents in England and worry that German bombs will fall on their houses.

Bill, Laura, and Eunice Campbell, just before they
left for northern British Columbia, 1942.

Today we heard on the radio that the British have surrendered Hong Kong, and many Canadians have been captured. Now Japan is at war with Canada. Will bombs drop on us too?

My father was a soldier in the last war, so he's too old to fight in this one. Once Christmas is over, he'll be itching to get back to the bush; for him, that means anything north of North Bay. He's a civil engineer, a road builder, and he was away for most of last year. I can tell he's already restless. For the hundredth time, he will try to please Mum with small gestures and magnificent promises that can't take away her loneliness. And then he will leave us again to go north by himself.

"I've found a new house for you here in Toronto, Laura," he told my mother last night. "It will be just right for the three of you."

"Not this time," she said. "I've had enough. We're going with you."

Westbound Train
July 1942
We are travelling more than three thousand miles to a road construction camp in northern British Columbia. Our old train rattles side to side, day after day, and sometimes I wonder if it is moving forward at all.

This is one long, tiresome trip. We stop at every little station to pick up more soldiers, more duffel bags, more cigarette smoke. As we wait at a standstill on some railway siding, more troop trains roar past us. Our new home is still very far away.

Dad left early in the spring with my mother's firm instructions to find us any place at all as long as it was *in the camp with him.* She put our house up for sale, stored our furniture, packed our clothes and belongings, and shipped them out to Dad. As soon as I finished Grade 10 exams, Mum and Bill and I marched into Union Station, clutching our train tickets. Destination: the middle of nowhere.

If Mum has any worries, she doesn't let us know it.

To pass the time on the train, Bill and I play cards, read books, or eat what's left of the food that Mum packed for the trip. Every hour or two, we visit poor Gyp in his cage in the baggage car and try to calm our dog's whimpers. Behind us, Mum talks to the soldiers' wives who are going west to join their husbands too. When we run out of conversation, we stare out the window at the wheat fields as the train hums *Saskatchewan . . . Saskatchewan . . . Saskatchewan.*

At night, the porter brings blankets and transforms our double seats into beds. I sleep in the bottom berth with Mum, and my brother climbs the little ladder to the top berth. He is almost too excited to sleep.

Today in the dining car, Bill unfolded a railway schedule and traced his finger down the long column of cities, towns, and arrival times along our route to our destination. Winnipeg. Saskatoon. Edmonton. Jasper. Prince George. Smithers . . .

"Here it is!" he said. "It says Skeena City right here!"

He grabbed the arm of the passing porter. "Have you ever stopped at a place called Skeena City, sir? That's where we're going. What's that place like?"

The porter looked down at my brother and grinned.

"Why, sure I've been there, son! It's a great, big city with tall skyscrapers and lots of movie theatres and nightclubs. More traffic in that town than Montreal, I'd say. And you should see the bright, neon lights!"

I heard a soldier snicker behind me. My brother didn't.

On the Train
Four Days Later

A few days ago, I woke up to see the Rocky Mountains for the first time in my life. I felt like I was dreaming with my eyes open. After we left Jasper, the train turned slowly north and curved through deep forests into a different mountain range. For two days the locomotive hugged high mountain ledges and chugged through rocky tunnels. Bill and I started to count the bears on the cliffs and the eagles soaring above them. Back in the baggage car, Gyp whimpered for freedom.

We have been following the Skeena River for a long, long time . . .

Then, this morning, a big surprise! The train stopped, and my father jumped aboard! He had hitchhiked to Smithers to travel the last leg of our journey with us. "We're almost there," he told us. "You are going to love it!"

At last, the locomotive groaned to a stop. A porter pulled the door open. We looked out at our new home. "No city," my brother whispered. Only a tiny white train station. Beyond that? Trees.

Skeena, BC
July 1942

"Welcome to Skeena," my father said with a grin.

We walked across the railway tracks, past the railway siding, and over a little creek on a bridge of rough wooden planks. My mother peered into the trees. Bill ran ahead, too excited to wait a minute longer.

"It's a tent!" he yelled over his shoulder.

It was a wall tent, actually. It had a wood plank floor and low wooden walls, with a heavy canvas tent over the top for a roof. No windows. Inside we found a wood-burning cook stove, a table with four chairs, and a high stand with pails for drinking water and washing water. Dad had stacked empty dynamite boxes so we could store our food, dishes, books, and clothes. Bill and I would sleep in a homemade bunk bed, and my parents had a double bed behind a curtain.

Rolling up her sleeves, Mum said, "This will work out just fine."

We have no bathroom, of course, only an outhouse back in the trees. We haul water from the creek to wash our clothes. As for taking a bath, Mum heats our bathwater in pots on the wood stove, then fills a large tin tub. We take turns as everybody else waits outside. I get the first bath, then Mum, then Bill, and then my poor dad takes the fourth bath in the lukewarm water.

We have plenty of good food to eat. The cook up at the work camp sends us eggs, milk, meat, tinned fruit and vegetables, and sometimes pie. Every morning Mum makes a fresh batch of homemade bread at the table. It is almost always delicious, but sometimes it refuses to rise. "Wartime yeast!" she mutters when she pulls a flat brick out of the cook stove. She doesn't want anybody to see her failed loaves at the dump behind the camp, so Bill and I carry them to the Kyex bridge and throw them down to the barking seals. They have quite an appetite for duds.

Every morning, Dad walks down the railroad tracks to the construction camp, which we mostly stay away from. The road workers sleep in five big bunkhouses, with nothing in them but rows of wooden bunk beds. They eat in a cookhouse in the middle of the camp, and the two cooks store their food safely from the bears in a special shed. Two rough cabins serve as offices. One is for the road contractor, Mr. Rayner, and one is for the government engineer, my dad.

Hundreds of men are living in these construction camps all along the Skeena River. Dad says they are working long hours, in the rain and mud, to build a decent road through the mountains to Prince Rupert so Canadian army trucks can reach the coast if Japan invades Canada. Everyone is worried. They need to work faster and faster.

Our camp is full of huge bulldozers, trucks, road-building equipment, and exhausted men. Only two other women live here, besides my mother.

Bill and I are the only kids.

September 1942

Nothing about Skeena is the same as Toronto. It's hard to believe the two places are in the same country. Take school, for example.

Mum and Dad took us into Prince Rupert on a little train we call the Skunk so we could register in school. I was supposed to start Grade 11, and Bill would start Grade 7. Mum had heard about a woman who took kids from the bush into her boarding house during the week and sent them home on the Skunk on the weekends.

We knocked on her door. A tall woman showed us around the damp boarding house. She wasn't surly, but it would be a stretch to call her warm-hearted. Mum looked out the window while the landlady recited a list of rules and instructions for boarding children.

"Remember to send your daughter into town with aprons, as she'll be helping with the housework around here," she said with her hands on her hips.

That was the end of that. We jumped back on the Skunk and returned to Skeena.

Somebody at the camp told us that BC has an excellent correspondence school for students in remote areas. Last week we received our first parcel of textbooks, along with personal letters from our teachers.

Dear Eunice,

I hope you are enjoying your new life in our province. I know you have moved a long way across Canada, so your new life must seem strange to you at times. Do you go for walks along the Skeena River? What do you think of our rainforest?

In this parcel you will find textbooks for English, History, Math, French, Latin, and Science. Try to find a place in your home where you can work by yourself. Keep regular school hours if possible, and take short breaks between each subject. Don't let yourself fall behind. Help your brother if you can. If you see that he's getting restless, go for a walk or eat a snack.

Each lesson will come to you on the train in an envelope. Complete the lesson and send it back to me. I know you don't have a telephone up there, so just send me your questions in a letter, and I'll be happy to answer.

What kind of books do you like to read? What are your interests and hobbies? Your first assignment is to tell me all about yourself in a long letter.

I look forward to being your English teacher. Once again, welcome to British Columbia, Eunice. I will wait for your interesting reply . . .

What a friendly teacher! I sat down immediately and wrote a long letter to him in a fresh notebook.

Thank you for your warm welcome. I already love northern British Columbia so much I never want to leave it.

I'm writing to you at my new desk. Some workers built us a small cabin so we'd be warm this winter. It looks like a palace compared to our old wall tent, but it's not too big. I have my own tiny room with a bunk, a desk, and a wood stove. My brother Bill sleeps in a kind of hallway, and he has his own desk too.

In our small front room, we have a cook stove and bench, our table and four chairs, a washing sink, and a cooking counter. My parents have a bedroom just big enough for their bed. And at last we have windows to look out at the trees!

You asked about my interests. Music makes me happy. I grew up in a family that likes to sing around the piano and listen to music on the radio. Back in Winnipeg, I started piano lessons when I was nine. At first I didn't like to practise, but after awhile I began to love playing piano pieces by Bach and Mozart. When we moved to Toronto, I found a weekend job at the Simpsons' department store. I spent all my wages on tickets to concerts, recitals, and ballets.

Do you know what kind of music I like best? Opera. (Do you hate opera? I hope not.) Our Toronto neighbour, Henry Bowen, asked me over to his house to listen to broadcasts from La Scala or London or Vienna on his short-wave radio. He explained all the stories to me. By the time I was fifteen, I was hooked on the Saturday afternoon radio broadcasts of the Metropolitan Opera. I never miss one.

Up here in Skeena, we have no piano, and no record player or records, but we do have a radio. To improve the reception, we put the radio on a high shelf made out of an old dynamite box. Every Saturday, I climb up on a chair and twist the dial until I hear the faraway voice of Milton Cross saying, "Good afternoon, opera lovers from coast to coast, welcome to the Metropolitan Opera, live from New York, brought to you by Texaco . . ."

I stand on that chair for the full two hours, with my ear up against the radio. One Saturday, I was listening to La Traviata between bursts of static when Mr. Rayner came to visit. He is the contractor for the road crew. He is a very kind friend who suffers from a terrible disease of the spine; he is almost completely bent over.

One glance up at me, and Mr. Rayner could see how much I loved opera, and how much I missed my music. He hatched a secret plan.

First, I received a mysterious parcel from Vancouver. I opened it to find a book, *The Opera: A History of its Creation and Performance, 1600–1941.*

A few weeks later, a freight train arrived from the east with a huge wooden crate amid a shipment of road-building equipment on a flatbed car. With great difficulty, several brawny men carried the crate across the railway siding and into the woods to our cabin. It was my upright Heintzman piano! I plan to give many concerts for Mr. Rayner, and I'm also going to take the Skunk into Prince Rupert soon for piano lessons with Miss Way.

Aside from music, I love listening to the wolves howl at night . . . reading *Wuthering Heights,* or any book by Sir Walter Scott, like *Lady of the Lake* or *Ivanhoe,* or any book by Charles Dickens . . . walking on the railway track and riverbank with my mother and brother and our dog Gyp . . . picnics on the rocks on the other side of Kyex bridge . . . watching for eagles, bears, ravens, and seals.

I promise to send my English assignments on time. I'm sorry this letter has been so long. I am a bit lonely.

Sincerely,

Eunice Campbell

Skeena, BC
November 1942

It has rained every single day for three weeks. A cold, hard rain.

My brother pulls on his raincoat and rubber boots, and goes out with my father to visit the other construction crews along the line. With cups of hot tea beside us, my mother and I read every library book that comes to us on the train. We listen to the radio to pass the time.

The war news is discouraging. The CBC says many Canadian soldiers were killed or captured at a place called Dieppe in France in August, but still we don't know how many. When I go on the train for a piano lesson in Prince Rupert, I walk through streets crowded with Canadian and American soldiers. It is more like an army camp than a town.

While my dad and the other men build the war road, Mum and I work on our own quiet war effort through long afternoons in our cabin—with pens, airmail paper, and postage stamps. My mother writes to my grandmother in England. She is taking care of a little girl named Helen who was shipped out of London during the Blitz. I write to three different men overseas: one in the Canadian army in India, one a navy pilot in South Africa, and one in the British navy. I tell them why I love this wilderness, and why I want to stay here.

We wait day after day for the mail. High in the mountains to the east of us, snowslides cover the railway tracks—and that means no trains, and no letters.

Mum stands at the window, staring out at the rain and mist. My father is hard at work. She is alone too much, and often silent. I worry about her.

Skeena, BC
May 1943

I have been on two boat rides, one a mystery to me.

On a cold, rainy morning, my father, his helper Fred, and another man from the camp took me along on their exploring trip up the Kyex, a spawning river for the salmon. We had to steer the motorboat around floating logs that were sticking out of the water, and through several rapids. When we stopped on shore, Fred managed to start a fire and boil hot water in a pail. He threw in a handful of loose tea. The men hiked along the riverbank.

I sat on a wet log in the mist, looking around, and loving my solitude. A mug of tea has never tasted so good.

It was my second boat trip that filled me with questions. Travelling in a small ferry, we crossed the widest part of the Skeena River, near the place where it flows into the Pacific, to a fishing village on the opposite bank.

For a morning, I walked past empty houses with boarded-up windows. Nobody seemed to be around. We entered a little schoolhouse. The door wasn't locked. I found books on the desks and pens, pencils, and dried-up ink. Papers lay scattered across the desks, and on the floor. Where were the students? Where was their teacher? Was this a ghost town?

My father told me that the RCMP had come to this village and taken the people away, even the kids, in big trucks—because of the war. I asked him where the police had taken these people. He shrugged. I don't think he knew.

As we closed the door behind us, a raven swooped low over the schoolhouse and flew out past the fishing boats to the wide river beyond.

This war is moving everyone to new places, I thought. How could a war so terrible bring me to a place that I love with all my heart?

What do we know for sure?

Eunice Campbell lived beside a road construction camp near the Skeena River in northern British Columbia from July 1942 until December of 1943.

"I remember crying as our train left the little white station opposite the camp," she said. "I was the only one in the family

99

who would miss the place. For years after, I could remember the mists hanging over the river, blue in the distance, and the smell of the pine and spruce trees that surrounded my life there.

"I still cherish the memories of my few months in Skeena and always felt they shaped me into the woman I became."

The Second World War uprooted thousands of families around the world. In Canada, more than one million men and women enlisted in the military in a country that had only 12 million citizens in 1939. Thousands of civilians travelled back and forth across the country to work on defence projects. Many kids didn't see their fathers for years after the war began, and some parents never came home.

During the long years of war, 44,093 Canadians in the armed forces lost their lives. Many others suffered physical and psychological injuries that lasted a lifetime.

After Japan bombed Pearl Harbour in Hawaii in 1941, and occupied the Aleutian Islands, Canada and the United States began to fear a Japanese invasion of North America through the northwest coast. Both governments needed to ship soldiers and munitions to northern British Columbia and Alaska. At that time northern Canadians depended on older trains, riverboats, and small bush planes for transportation. They had poor roads—and in most places, no roads at all.

Thousands of Canadians began to work quickly on three important projects in northern Canada.

The largest and most difficult project was the Alcan Military Highway—a gravel road across 2,333 kilometres of rugged wilderness from Dawson Creek, BC, through Yukon Territory to Delta Junction, Alaska. Despite tremendous hardships, eleven thousand American soldiers and sixteen thousand Canadian and American civilians managed together to build the road in less than eight months. Now paved, it is usually called the Alaska Highway or Alcan Highway and remains an important route for northerners.

The second project was the CANOL pipeline, a questionable plan to bring oil from Norman Wells, NWT, across the Mackenzie Mountains to Whitehorse, Yukon. More than twenty thousand workers completed that difficult project in less than two years. A shortage of Arctic clothing forced some of them to burn lumber and bridge timbers to stay warm. Despite their hardships, they built 2600 kilometres of pipelines, 830 kilometres of winter gravel roads and telephone lines, 2400 of winter roads, and ten aircraft landing strips.

Unfortunately, the pipeline never worked well, and the project cost five times more than original estimates. Oil flowed through the pipeline for only thirteen months before it was abandoned, leaving behind what some historians called a "junkyard monument to military stupidity." The junk is still there. Hikers and hunters use the route to reach wilderness.

Finally, the Canadian government decided to build an unpaved road through the difficult mountain passes between Prince George and Prince Rupert, BC. Work on the road began in March 1942, with hundreds of workers in construction camps along the railway tracks that followed the Skeena River. The Skeena Highway opened on September 4, 1944.

All of these projects required hard work and many sacrifices, not only from the construction workers themselves, but also from their spouses and children.

Bill Campbell in the bush at Skeena, BC, 1942.
COURTESY OF CAMPBELL FAMILY COLLECTION

Eunice and Bill Campbell were among the many northern children who studied by correspondence. The province of British Columbia developed Canada's first correspondence system for children in remote areas. The first parcels of books and lessons went out in 1919 to thirteen children who lived in lighthouses. Teachers in the south often developed a friendly pen-pal relationship with northern students who might be isolated or lonely. Families could also order library books by mail.

The Skeena River runs through the traditional territory of many First Nations, including the Tsimshian, the Gitxsan, and the Nisga'a. At the time the road was built through their territory, the Canadian government did not recognize their aboriginal rights, or consult them properly about their own wishes. Today, with new land agreements, they have a say in all decisions about development in their territory.

Many Japanese Canadian fishing families also made their home along the Skeena River before the Second World War. These Japanese Canadians suffered unfair punishment in the panic of war, and the racism of the time, even though they were loyal to Canada. In February 1942, Prime Minister Mackenzie King and his cabinet decided that all twenty thousand Japanese Canadians in BC, including sixteen thousand who had been born in Canada, must leave their homes and belongings behind on the coast. The RCMP and military took these men, women, and children away from their homes on short notice and put them in prison camps in the Interior.

Eunice Campbell visited one of the abandoned Japanese Canadian villages along the Skeena River in 1943. "I was an inexperienced and immature young girl, completely brainwashed by war news from the press, and by biased, racist people around me," she remembers. "We thought as we were told to think, and that kind of blind nationalism could only happen in wartime."

She said she couldn't remember hearing one adult disagree with the internment policy at the time. "Later in life, I came to feel very badly about not speaking out about the injustice."

After the war ended, Japanese Canadians were given the choice to either move to Japan or move east of the Rocky Mountains.

The government did not release the last interned Japanese Canadians until April 1, 1949, four years after the war ended. In 1988 the Canadian government apologized formally to the Japanese Canadians for this mistreatment.

After a tearful goodbye to Skeena, Eunice Campbell moved back to Toronto with her family in early 1944. Five years later, she married Emile Goyette and began to raise a family of five children, encouraging them to love music, nature, and Canada. Now eighty-four years old, she continues to enjoy Metropolitan Opera broadcasts every single Saturday afternoon. I am proud to call her my mother.

Why Kids Love Moosehide

Angie Joseph, age eleven
Moosehide, Yukon, 1957

I live with my family in a village near the mountains of the northern Yukon. Why is it called Moosehide? A long time ago, a landslide scooped a wide curve out of the side of our mountain. People said it looked like a moose hide, and the name stayed with the place. If you follow a trail over the hill, you will find us.

We live in log houses that our parents and grandparents built themselves. The Yukon River flows right past our front door. We have forests, creeks, ponds, and high hills behind us, and all around us. Each house in Moosehide has many kids in it. We have known each other since we were babies. Nobody is lonely here, because nobody is a stranger.

Yesterday I stood at the top of the hill with everybody I love— kids, parents, aunties and uncles, the elders—watching huge chunks of melting ice smashing and crashing against each other. We listened to the c-r-e-a-k-i-n-g sound of the ice breaking up in the river. Like everybody else, I knew what that meant.

It is the sound of spring coming to Moosehide.

The sun is warm on my face. Maybe today the Yukon River will push the biggest block of winter ice to the shore, so the water can flow freely past us on its way to our cousins in Eagle, Alaska.

"Or maybe tomorrow," says my sister Julia.

"Or maybe the next day," says my sister Loretta.

When Grandma McLeod hears any kid in Moosehide talking about spring breakup, she gives the same warning.

"Don't go anywhere near the river without us," she said last

The kids of Moosehide with their teacher at spring breakup.
Angie Joseph is the girl with her hands in her pockets.
Left to right, on top of ice: Virginia Joseph, Eileen Henry, Margaret Henry, and George Semple. Left to right, bottom: Lota Semple, Danny Joseph, Lorette Joseph, Julia Joseph, Angie Joseph. Rear: Johnny Semple in front of teacher Mabel Gosbee, William Henry, Richard Semple, Victor Henry, and John Semple.

week. "You can go rambling around the bush anywhere you like with me, but stay away from the river when you're alone. Don't let me see you do it."

You can't get away with anything in this place. If my mother doesn't catch us, then Annie Henry will see us, or Grandma McLeod, or some other auntie or uncle on the lookout for kids wading into a cold, rushing river in rubber boots. They would scoop us out of the water faster than a fish can swim.

We want spring so much we can hardly think about anything else.

We want to follow the creeks with our rubber boots sinking into the squishy mud. We want to look for frogs near the slough, and slide down the slippery grass on the hill. I want to search for sweet roots that Grandma McLeod needs. We want to go fishing by Big Rock and make holes in the soft spring ice. I could sit there all day long, waiting for the greyling to bite the bait, while I listen to my brother's jokes.

The sun will get warmer and warmer. Deep snow will trickle away into the creeks.

At the end of May, on Memorial Day, all the people in Moosehide walk up the hill to the graveyard, to clean the weeds away from the graves and make everything look good. Fathers and grandfathers rake away the brush. Mothers and grandmothers bring good food for us to eat. Kids run around in circles, chasing each other. And then we sit on the grass all together for the biggest picnic of the year. Bannock with raisins. Dried salmon. Meat sandwiches. Hot tea. Cookies and cake.

This is the taste of summer coming to Moosehide. The most delicious tastes are waiting for us up on the hill in the bush.

"Let's go!" Grandma McLeod will say one hot July morning, and she'll grab her rifle just in case we meet a bear in the berry patch. All the kids in Moosehide follow her, carrying lard pails into the woods.

Each week of summer brings different berries in different places. Sweet blueberries. Red cranberries. We know where to look. It isn't a secret. We eat berries as quickly as we pick them, but the older kids can fill a pail in no time at all.

And then the best time of summer begins. For a few days, we notice that the grown-ups are too busy to look sideways at us. Every day they pack our summer food, our summer clothes, our summer tent frames, and other belongings into the boats.

"You stay here and watch the little ones, Angie," my mother tells me. "We need to go soon, and we're not ready yet."

Every kid in Moosehide jumps with excitement. Fish camp! We stand on the riverbank and watch the grown-ups go over and come back, go over and come back.

Kids are the last ones to climb into the boats and go across the river. While our parents set up the wall tents, the fishing wheels, the fish drying racks, and the smokehouses, we play through every day.

In the cool mornings, we chase each other around the camp and along the riverbank in a game of Tag that lasts from one day to the next. We play Hide and Seek inside and outside of the boats. *Ready or not, here I come!* My sister Julia likes to explore the crumbling wreck of a huge, old steamboat on the riverbank to see what she can find under the tangled weeds and rotten boards.

The sun gets hotter and hotter. In the afternoon, we sit in the shade of a big tree and carve driftwood or bits of tree bark into little boats, with motor propellers at the back, and a pole and string for pulling them on the water. We carve willow whistles.

"Come and help us now," Grandma McLeod says. The grown-ups don't tell us how to catch fish, or how to dry fish on racks, or how to hang it in the smokehouse. We are supposed to watch them to learn. They give us little fish to work on. When we get restless, we can go.

One day last summer, we decided to walk through the bush to visit old Mr. Laurence at his cabin. We found the friendly old man sitting outside his front door.

Mr. Laurence has lived by himself forever, and you can tell. The only window in his log cabin is so grimy you can't see through the glass. His table is cluttered with pots and pans and the left-overs of last month's lunch. He probably uses 1923 newspapers as kindling in his woodstove.

"Lucky me! I have visitors!" he said in his frog-croaky voice. "Come inside, and eat Johnny cake!"

"Don't eat it," Julia whispered to me.

"Don't eat it," I whispered over my shoulder to Loretta.

"Don't eat it," Loretta whispered back to the kids behind her on the path.

Every kid in Moosehide knows that Mr. Laurence's Johnny cake is old, old, old bannock as dry as the dust on the old man's boots. Who knows how ancient he is? Maybe he cooked up that Johnny cake in his greasy frying pan a century ago.

"How about berries instead, Mr. Laurence?"

I asked the question because I love the answer.

Alone in the bush, the old man makes his own kind of summer ice cream. He picks soapberries when they're ripe, and mashes them down with a stick in a pot. Then he whips up the mixture until it is nice and red and foamy. After that he stirs in lots and lots and lots of white sugar. Fortunately, soapberries don't taste like soap. They're as sweet as July.

We ate our special ice cream with Mr. Laurence, then said goodbye and wandered home to eat a good fish dinner around the campfire. Do you know our summer sun never sets? Near midnight, it goes down just a few minutes, but a warm glow stays in the sky. We can see the sun and the moon almost at the same time. We have no night, no darkness—only sunlight and campfires, cool water and woodsmoke.

We stay at fish camp all of July and most of August, until it is time to cross the river again and go home. Then we hear the sound of Moosehide in the fall.

■ ■ ■

One September morning, a big kid in Moosehide pulls the rope on the church bell. *Ding, dong, ding, dong.* Kids race out the door of their houses and run towards a tall log school near the riverbank. My dad built an addition on the school so that we would have a bit more room.

When we walk inside the front door, we find a playroom with new games, small toys, and books waiting for us. Then we go through another doorway into our classroom. Waiting for us is Mrs. Mable Gosbee, our teacher. She tried to be stern when she first arrived here in Moosehide, but we taught her how to laugh. We can tell she likes us now.

Mrs. Gosbee sleeps in one room of the log school, and she has a kitchen behind it where she can cook for herself. On cool fall days, she gets up early in the morning to light the woodstove in our classroom so we will be warm when we read. She lights two gas lamps so we can see what we're doing. Sometimes she loses her temper with us, but she knows how to be kind.

All the kids from Grade 1 to Grade 6 share the same classroom. Big kids sit in the back, and little ones sit at the front. I'm right in the middle. From our wooden desks, we can look out one large window, facing the hill. We can look out another large window, facing the river. We want to go *out, out, out* as soon as possible— sooner than recess, right now—and Mrs. Gosbee knows it!

On rainy or extra-cold days—even on Saturdays and holidays and in the evenings—she opens the school so we can play Checkers or Snakes and Ladders in the playroom. When I'm by myself, I like to read books. Sometimes our teacher takes us to some small rooms upstairs to sew quilts or do some artwork.

"Do you think your dad would come in and play his fiddle for the class?" Mrs. Gosbee asked me one day. And the next thing you know, my dad was right in the middle of our class, teaching us how to dance the Virginia reel, and how to play the guitar, the piano, and the fiddle.

My dad's fiddle music is the sound of winter coming to Moosehide.

■ ■ ■

We have an old dance hall in our village. We have feasts there, and the kids are allowed to roller skate inside when it's empty. On the night of the big dance last year, my mother and other women

Berry-picking with Grandma McLeod on a hot summer day.

in Moosehide brought homemade cake and other treats to the hall. I could smell coffee perking as people came in the door. We stayed up late, running around the edges of the hall as the older ones danced jigs to the fiddle music.

"It's time for you kids to go home now," my mother said to us.

"I want to stay for cake," said Julia.

"Me too," I said.

"And me too," said Loretta.

Munching sweet cake, we walked home through soft, falling snow. In the morning we woke up to go sledding. Every kid in Moosehide has a sled. Our fathers made them for us. These wooden sleds have sharp, steel runners at the bottom, so we can slide down the hill at top speed. Sometimes our dogs pull us for a ride on our toboggans.

A soft snowfall can become a snowstorm and grow bigger into a blizzard. Winter darkness comes soon. For a few months, the darkness stays with us all day and night, except for a few hours around noon when the sun glows over the hills.

Winter pushes its long, icy fingers through the cracks between the logs in the houses, touching the elders on the shoulders. Kids in Moosehide know what to do. Nobody tells us. We go and fetch the wood from the woodpile. We split it with an axe near the door. We bring the wood in our arms to the elders' houses. "Here's some bannock with raisins in it," said Grandma McLeod. "And now I have time for a story . . ."

As soon as the Yukon River is frozen, my dad walks out on the ice and chops a deep hole—big enough so we can dip our water buckets through it. He carries water containers back to our house. My mother pours the river water through cheesecloth to clean it, and then she boils it in a big pot. Clean water from the Yukon River makes the best tea in the world.

The taste of hot, sugary tea on a cold winter night means that Christmas is coming to Moosehide.

■ ■ ■

The first sign of Christmas is when I find my mother and her best friend, Annie Henry, sewing while they sip tea together. Annie sews the soft hide into new slippers, with rabbit fur around the ankles. My mother sews a thousand shining beads—red and blue and yellow—to make flowers to decorate each slipper. Every year they make our Christmas presents together.

After Christmas, we go back to school for long, slow winter months until the caribou herds tell us spring is almost here. We see the grown-ups packing again. We're getting ready to go out on the land for the hunt. At school we get a bit twitchy in our desks. *Time to go. Time to go.*

"But, but, but . . ." Mrs. Gosbee used to say. Now she knows better. She can only wave goodbye as we run out the door to join the caribou hunt.

The snow melts. The sun climbs in the sky. One day everyone is back on the top of this hill in Moosehide again, watching the river and waiting.

We ask Grandma McLeod when the spring breakup will come, and when the river will be free again.

"Maybe today. Maybe tomorrow. Maybe the day after that."

What do we know for sure?

Angie Joseph-Rear told me that whenever she wants to feel happy, she closes her eyes and thinks about her life in Moosehide when she was a kid.

"I can take myself right back to the creek, just thinking about it," she says.

Today Angie is the Hän Language Programmer for the Tr'ondëk Hwëch'in First Nation. Her job is to listen carefully to elders and help to preserve the traditional language of her people. When we talked about Moosehide, she taught me how to say, "How are you?" in Hän. *N'änjit Dähònch'e?*

Born in 1946, Angie was one of the middle daughters of

Joe and Susan Joseph. Altogether, the Joseph family raised five girls and three boys in the close-knit community. Every kid in Moosehide called the elder Mary McLeod "Grandma McLeod." An important street is named after her in Dawson City, and people still remember her stories.

Today Angie lives in Dawson City, but her family loves to spend the summer in their cabin at Moosehide. Nearby is the old log school where she used to go. People take good care of it. Every two years, the Tr'ondëk Hwëch'in have a special gathering, like a giant family reunion, called the Moosehide Gathering.

It has been a long, difficult journey back to Moosehide for Angie and her friends, a journey that required a lot of courage. It will take time to tell you why.

The story begins a long, long time before Angie was born.

In 1857 the Canadian government decided that all First Nations children in Canada should be taken away from their families, and educated in schools away from home. Different Christian churches ran the schools across Canada. In 1910 the Anglican Church built the Chooutla Residential School in Carcross, Yukon—about six hundred kilometres south of Moosehide—and the Tr'ondëk Hwëch'in children were sent to live in this boarding school. You will read more about this school in the next chapter.

The Choutla School in Carcross, Yukon, burned down in 1939.

For a few short years, between 1948 and 1957, children in Moosehide were allowed to go to school in their home village again.

Angie was one of these lucky ones. For the first ten years of her life, she was a kid during this special time. However, in the late summer of 1957, when Angie was eleven years old, she and the other children of Moosehide received a terrible surprise. They found out that Mrs. Gosbee would not be their teacher anymore. Their tall log school would be closed. Their lives were about to change forever.

Nobody had warned them.

One day a big truck arrived. All the children, including Angie, had to climb in the back of the truck. They had no choice. They had to wave goodbye to their parents in Moosehide and travel south to Carcross to live in a big residential school.

The next story is about what happened in Carcross.

Runaway

Ronald Johnson, age fifteen
Chooutla Residential School, Carcross, Yukon, 1957

I ran away from this jail of a school with Donny, and Walter, and George. We were senior boys, and we'd been planning our getaway for about a month.

We have a short church service at the school every day, and you have to line up before that. And us four boys, we stayed towards the back end of the line. When the line began to move to go to the service, that's when we dashed out behind the play-room door.

We had all this planned out beforehand, because we had our coats and boots ready up the stairway there.

Out the door we went! We walked through the bush, climbed a little hill, and we crossed the highway. Then we went across country. We were trying to get home.

We walked in single file. It was late November, and the snow was about three or four feet deep. We took turns breaking trail. We came to Dominion Highway, the highway that goes to Whitehorse, and crossed over. We broke a little tree down, and one of us pulled that tree behind us to cover our boot tracks. And we walked on the railroad track for about five miles. About a mile up the track, we saw a train coming. We jumped in the bush to hide until the train passed us.

It was getting to be late afternoon. We kept walking. In the distance we saw a bonfire. There were some railway workers fixing the railroad track. They called us over. They were having coffee break then, and they spotted us.

Residential school students in a truck outside Whitehorse parish hall. Tr'ondek Hwëch'in children rode more than six hundred kilometres in the same truck to reach Chooutla Residential School in Carcross, Yukon.

"We're going have to turn you boys in," one guy said. "If it was summertime, we would let you go. Not in this type of weather. It's going to get cold tonight."

So I guess this guy had a portable phone. He clicked it to the telephone wire and made a call, maybe to the RCMP or to the school. A little while later, the school truck pulled up, and they took us in.

The four of us were scared about what was going to happen to us. I guess we knew what it might be. So they took us back to the school. They made us take a shower, and they gave us clean clothes, then we got strapped with a leather belt. And then they took our shoes away.

"You will not be allowed outside for a month," the principal said. That's why they took our shoes, so we couldn't run. It was winter.

And then, the staff gave the four of us different places in that school that we had to scrub for a month with a toothbrush. Me and my friend got the auditorium—it's a huge room. After school every day after our other chores—like washing dishes in the kitchen and peeling potatoes—we had to get down on our hands and knees and scrub that big floor with soapy water and the toothbrush. And we done that for a month. The other boys did the main floor of the school, or the staircase. That's a three-story building. And that staircase, it's made out of concrete. Kneeling on that concrete to scrub the stairs for hours, it hurt.

So that was our punishment for running away. Two of my buddies ran away a second time. They made it as far as Mayo before they got caught. I don't know how they done it.

I'm not proud I ran away, and I'm not sorry I did. We done it. We paid for it.

What do we know for sure?

You can learn how First Nations children and teenagers felt about residential schools in Canada by how often they tried to run away.

Ronald Johnson and his friends were prepared to walk all the way home—six hundred kilometres—through deep snow in a cold winter just to escape residential school in the late 1950s.

I met Ronald at the Dänojà Zho Cultural Centre in Dawson City, Yukon, on an important day. He had come to celebrate the publication of a book about the brave Tr'ondëk Hwëch'in kids who lived through many years of residential school, and severe punishment and abuse, to put their lives back together again.

About ten years ago, a small group of former residential school students started to meet in Dawson City to help each other with their problems. They called themselves the K'änächá group, which means "taking care of each other" in the Hän language. On May 17, 2007, the Tr'ondëk Hwëch'in First Nation held a Welcome Home Ceremony to help the grown-up residential school students and their families heal from their hard experiences.

The former students made a scrapbook together, filled with pictures and stories about the residential school system. They published their scrapbook in a book called Tr'ëhuhch'in Näwtr'udäh'a. In English, the title is *Finding Our Way Home.*

Ronald published his own story in the book. I asked him if I could visit him at his house to hear more of the story of how he ran away. We sat in his kitchen on a winter afternoon, and he told me more about the escape, such as the first names of his friends, and what happened to each boy later in life. He agreed to allow me to reprint his original story, and the extra details I wrote in my notebook, so you could read it too.

I used his exact words. I did not add anything that I imagined to this story.

Ronald grew up in a large family of ten children on the site of the original Tro'chek seasonal camp. "My dad was a wood-cutter and a self-taught person," he remembers. "We had a pretty good life."

Like Angie Joseph-Rear and other people who grew up at Moosehide, Ronald remembers the long, bumpy ride to the Yukon Residential School in Carcross in the back of the big truck. The trip took more than seven hours.

"At that time, the Klondike Highway was a rough gravel road," he remembers. "By the time we got to Carcross, we had so much dust on us, we looked like ghosts."

It didn't take Ronald very long to decide that he wanted to escape the huge residential school. "We just wanted to get away from that place, and its rules and regulations. The rules were pretty strict. The girls and boys were kept separate, in different parts of the building, so even if you got caught talking to your sister, you would get punished."

He compared the school to a prison, "except that the prisoners in jail got more freedom than we did. Children were crying for their parents. They were homesick, and they couldn't even talk to their brothers and sisters."

The same thing happened to First Nations, Metis, and Inuit children all across Canada for more than a century.

Canada's first residential schools—special boarding schools for First Nations and Metis children, run by different Christian churches—opened after the government passed the Gradual Civilization Act in 1857. This law was an attempt to change Aboriginal people into "acceptable" Europeans. At that time, the government wanted tribal peoples to speak English, not their own languages; to read and write in English; and to become Christians, like most of the new settlers.

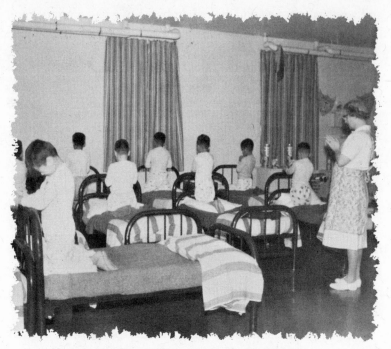

Boys saying their nightly prayers in the
dormitory at Chooutla Residential School.

The government decided to start with the children.

Churches sent missionaries—meaning religious preachers and teachers—to isolated First Nations villages and reserves all across Canada. Churches set up boarding schools to give First Nations children what they thought was a "proper" education. The children usually had to live far away from their families, friends, and relatives.

Many missionaries abused the children in their care with harsh physical punishment, humiliation, and sexual abuse.

It was a very hard and lonely time for thousands of First Nations children across Canada. Far from home, and homesick, many kids were mistreated. They didn't have enough good food to eat, and they were often sick. Many died, and they were buried in unmarked graves. They were severely punished if they spoke their own language, or if they tried to escape.

This suffering went on year after year, decade after decade.

Many First Nations families wanted their children to be educated, and they sent them to the residential schools willingly at first. Soon parents had no choice. In 1920 the Canadian government passed a law to make it compulsory for First Nations children between the ages of seven and fifteen to go to residential school. If parents refused, they could go to jail, and police would come to seize the children.

Children were allowed to visit their parents only at Christmas and in the summer, and sometimes not even then.

Missionary teachers taught the kids to reject their First Nation's spiritual beliefs. Educated for only part of the day, the children did not receive the quality of teaching that other Canadian kids received. After their classes, they had to clean the school, work in the kitchen and garden, chop wood, and do other jobs to keep the boarding school going. Often, they left school as teenagers with feelings of shame and worthlessness, and some even learned to hate themselves. When they went home to their communities, they didn't fit in very well.

The Chooutla Residential School in Carcross, Yukon, opened in 1910. Run by the Anglican Church, the building burned down in 1939, and most students lived in poor conditions in old buildings until a new residential school was built in 1954.

First Nations students in the Yukon attended that larger school in Carcross until it closed in 1969.

Former residential school students had some good times together—and some kids remember liking school—but every former student I have interviewed in any part of Canada has described suffering of some kind. Many older First Nations people remember hunger or poor food, bullying, beatings, severe punishment for small mistakes, humiliating insults, racism, and sexual abuse by staff members.

On June 11, 2008, Prime Minister Stephen Harper stood in the House of Commons and apologized on behalf of all Canadians to the First Nations, Metis, and Inuit citizens who attended residential schools, or lived with the consequences in their families.

"The treatment of children in Indian residential schools is a sad chapter in our history," said the prime minister. "Today we recognize that this policy of assimilation was wrong, has caused great harm, and has no place in our country."

The Canadian government organized the Truth and Reconciliation Commission to help Canadians understand what happened at the residential schools, and to heal the deep problems they left behind. You can learn more about this effort at www.trc-cvr.ca.

To learn more about what life was like for children in residential schools, visit the online resource *Where are the Children?* at www.wherearethechildren.ca.

Today Tr'ondëk Hwëch'in children go to a beautiful school in their own community—and their future looks much brighter.

The Tr'ondëk Hwëch'in government works to ensure the

children in its community receive an excellent education while maintaining their connections to traditional knowledge, their language, and their land.

Ronald Johnson now lives in Dawson City, Yukon. At fifty-nine, he has made a good life for himself, and he is happy again. I admire his resistance to unfair treatment, his long walk for justice, and most of all, his courage.

Letter to my Mother and Father

Davidie Pisurayak Kootook, age fourteen
Writing from the wreckage of a plane
Four hundred kilometres northwest of Yellowknife, NWT, 1972

Few days ago we got to Cambridge Bay. We were going to Yellowknife. The airplane fell.

When this happened Neemee died and the nurse. The pilot's legs are broken, he cannot walk. I am alright. We fell between Yellowknife and Cambridge Bay, on the hills.

In a few more days, on the fourteenth, the pilot wants me to walk to Yellowknife. So I must try and walk.

I pray to God that I will see you again. We eat all the time, the pilot and I. There is just two of us. We have white man's food (dried food). The food is in a box, the box is just a bit bigger than my red suitcase. The weather was bad yesterday and today is foggy.

Johnny Kovalah and Lena, give them a kiss for me. We cut wood with an axe and we make fire. There is just me and the pilot here. Neemee and the nurse died when the airplane fell. There were four of us.

I will see you again in Spence Bay or in Heaven. I try to pray. I do not feel cold in the daytime, only at nights. We have five thick sleeping bags: two of them we use for a tent and three to sleep in. And another one for a mattress.

Today we have been here four days. The pilot's legs are broken. I am fine. I can walk. Give Johnny Kovalah and Lena a kiss for me. Yellowknife is far away from here and I am going to try and walk there. The pilot wants me to walk there.

I am finishing writing now. I do not have any more writing paper.

Davidie Pessurajak Kootook

What do we know for sure?

Davidie Pisurayak Kootook wrote this letter to his parents before he died of starvation on December 1, 1972—twenty-three days after the plane crash. His message was found at the site of the plane wreckage.

The Inuk boy wrote the original letter in Inuktitut syllabics, a writing system of the Inuit of Nunavut and northern Quebec. This is the exact English translation of the note, which was entered as evidence at the court fatality inquiry after the accident. A translator read it aloud during the inquest.

Davidie was a boy of extraordinary courage. The story of his bravery during his final days is not as well known across Canada as I think it should be.

I found most of the information about him in newspaper articles about the fatality inquiry, and in *The Survivor*, an excellent book about the crash by Edmonton writer Peter Tadman.

Davidie Pisurayak Kootook grew up in a small village in the High Arctic. When he was a boy, his community was called Spence Bay, and it was inside the Northwest Territories. This area became part of the new territory of Nunavut in 1999. Now the village is called by its Inuit name, Taloyoak. (pronounced Ta-low-ywak)

In late 1972, Davidie became very ill with severe stomach pain and vomiting. Judy Hill, the nurse at the nursing station, arranged for an air ambulance flight—usually called a medivac flight, for medical evacuation—to get the boy to hospital in Yellowknife.

She suspected he had acute appendicitis and needed immediate surgery. She also sent another patient on the emergency flight. Davidie's twenty-five-year-old aunt, a woman named Neemee Nulliayok, was expecting a new baby, and she was having trouble with her pregnancy.

The nurse asked the pilot of a Twin Otter plane to take her and her two patients as far as Cambridge Bay. There they would try to find another airlift to Yellowknife.

Davidie was carefully placed in the plane beside his aunt and the nurse. The plane travelled to Cambridge Bay and landed safely, but the winter flying conditions were very bad. By coincidence, a pilot named Martin Hartwell had landed a different plane in Cambridge Bay a few hours earlier, after a trip with some mining engineers. He agreed to take the nurse and her two patients back to Yellowknife.

The twin-engine plane crashed into a hillside about eighty kilometres south of Great Bear Lake on November 8. Judy Hill died in the accident. Neemee Nulliayok suffered a broken back and died five hours later, as did her unborn baby girl, who was due to be born in one month. Martin Hartwell, the pilot, suffered two broken ankles and a broken knee, so he couldn't walk.

Although Davidie was very sick, he was not seriously injured in the crash. And so his heroic efforts began.

First, he tried to comfort his pregnant aunt and make her more comfortable before she died. Then he worked with the struggling pilot to build a rough tent with some sleeping bags, a pair of engine tarps, and a piece of the broken airplane.

The boy and the pilot were stranded in the wilderness in severe winter weather with temperatures that averaged around minus thirty-seven Celsius, but fell into the minus forties. They knew that cold was their biggest enemy. Davidie gathered wood and chopped enough wood to keep the fire going—day and night. He melted snow for drinking water.

Their emergency food ran out after ten days. Davidie began to collect Caribou moss, a kind of lichen plant that grows on rocks. He waded through waist-deep snow to try and catch fish in a nearby lake, but he caught nothing. It must have been so frustrating for him. Two herds of caribou—one with ten animals in it—roamed close to the plane wreck, but the boy had no gun to hunt them.

Finally, he went out on the land to search for any food that could keep them alive. He found lichens, spruce needles, wild cranberry leaves, carbonized berries, moss leaves, bark and wood. He suffered severe frostbite to his toes, lost thirty-five pounds, and finally couldn't walk anymore himself. In his final days, he spoke to the pilot about his parents and his brothers and sisters.

Davidie died sometime between the night of November 30 and the early morning of December 1. A rescue team found the crash site a week later. The pilot survived.

I think it is very important to remember what happened after Davidie died.

The boy's body was buried in Beechmount Cemetery in Edmonton, thousands of miles from his home, with only a church minister and two people present. There was no gravestone, and nothing to mark his name. He was immediately nominated for the Governor-General's Medal of Bravery, one of Canada's highest awards for the courage of ordinary citizens.

A year after the plane crash, the award had still not been made. Kiviaq, an Inuk city councillor in Edmonton known to most people at that time as David Ward, wrote to the Governor-General asking for the reason behind the delay.

"Is it because of his age, sex, or racial background?" he asked. Kiviaq then asked the City of Edmonton to properly mark the boy's grave. Two years later, this had still not been done. Kiviaq took action of his own. A simple flat marker over the grave says: *David Kootook, August 13, 1958–December, 1972.*

Nineteen years after Davidie's death, when Peter Tadman published his book about the accident, called *The Survivor*, the Governor-General's Medal for Bravery had still not been awarded to Davidie. Finally, in 1994, Canada awarded the Meritorious Service Cross to Kootook's family for his efforts as a civilian to save the pilot's life.

In 1998 Davidie's mother and family also proudly attended a special ceremony in Taloyoak to launch an Arctic ship called the David Pisurayak Kootook.

"Pisurayak Kootook is a true northern hero, and it is only fitting that he be recognized with this honour in his own community," Natlikmeot MLA John Ningark later told the Nunavut legislative assembly.

In Taloyoak, now home to more than eight hundred people, a plaque near the airport honours the young boy who did so much to save a life. Today, two hundred and forty kids in the community attend Netsilik School.

I think about one brave young northerner every time I walk past a stone inukshuk that was built in his honour in my own home city, Edmonton.

Remembering Davidie Pisurayak Kootook is a way to honour him too.

The Swimmer

Xavier Kataquapit, age six
Attawapiskat First Nation, 1982

One summer we adopted a scruffy one-year-old little mutt.
I was about six, and I don't even remember the dog's name.
One sunny day, Mom and Dad organized a family day trip out
to James Bay in our freighter canoe. We begged our parents
to bring our new pet along for the ride. We were headed to
Akimiski Island.

The trip in the large twenty-four-foot freighter canoe started
out well, but soon the large swells tossed us around on the water
and our four-legged friend began to bark, shake, and become
agitated. He kept looking over the side of the moving boat. We
tried our best to hold on to his homemade twine collar.

As we neared the mouth of the Attawapiskat River, the flowing, tea-coloured fresh water gave way to the churning, grey salty
ocean of James Bay. Suddenly our little pet leaped out of our
grasp and dived into the river!

Dad swung our fully loaded boat around and slowly
approached the swimming dog that was heading for the mainland. We reached out to grab his collar, but the rough water made
it difficult to get close, and every effort to push towards the dog
seemed to drive him further on.

It broke our hearts to watch the little dog bobbing among
the huge swells, and we felt helpless. He swam on and soon
we lost sight of him in the vastness of the great James Bay.
There was nothing to be done, so Dad continued our ride to
the island.

Xavier Kataquapit, eleven, and his younger brother Joseph, behind him, unpacking a snowmobile sled during the spring goose hunt on the Lakitusaki River. This is the traditional hunting territory of their mother Susan's family, the Paulmartins. The river runs through Polar Bear Provincial Park in northern Ontario.

COURTESY OF KATAQUAPIT FAMILY COLLECTION

We spent the day on Akimiski Island. We did our best to enjoy our time, but we had heavy hearts and worried minds with the image still fresh of that little dog lost on the bay. We all knew that it would be almost impossible for our little furry friend to survive the swim to land.

We also realized that even if he made it to shore, the poor mutt would be stranded in the midst of extreme wilderness. By the end of the day, we had accepted that our dog was gone for good.

We arrived back home late in the evening as the sun drew low on the horizon. We were tired and exhausted after a long day of salty fresh air, bright sun, and running on the pebble beaches of

Akimiski Island. The loss of our dog was still on our minds as we slowly unpacked the canoe and hauled our gear back to the house.

Suddenly, there was a familiar bark: up at our front door, we were astonished to see our little dog, alive and well and welcoming us back home! He was dry, but a little haggard looking and somewhat frantic. He had somehow managed to swim to the mainland and, to our surprise, cross a major creek, then find his way through ten kilometres of the most intense bush and wilderness back to our home in Attawapiskat.

Somehow this little mutt had survived against all odds, driven by such huge devotion to return to us. If he could have talked, what a story he would have told!

That dog had a special place in our hearts from that day forward. He didn't live long, but I think of him often and I thank him for teaching me a lesson about love and devotion.

What do we know for sure?

Up in the territory of the Mushwego Cree on the James Bay coast, everybody seems to know Xavier Kataquapit. I found his interesting stories everywhere I went!

This started to happen just before I climbed aboard a Creebec Air plane in Timmins, Ontario, heading north. I picked up a copy of the *Wawatay News*, an excellent First Nations newspaper, and found Xavier's column, "Under A Northern Sky." He has been writing a regular column since 1997, and it now appears in seven newspapers across the country. His stories have also been broadcast on the radio.

After I finished reading one story, somewhere in the clouds way above Moosonee, I opened the pages of *Nation* magazine, a publication of the James Bay Cree. I found another one of Xavier's stories and enjoyed it just as much.

Finally, the plane landed in Attawapiskat. At the airport, a friendly guy named Joseph Kataquapit gave me a lift to the Kataquapit Inn, where I planned to stay for a while.

"Any chance you're related to a writer named Xavier Kataquapit?" I asked.

"He's my brother!" Joseph replied. He handed me a CD full of Xavier's stories. I knew immediately I wanted to include one of the tales about his childhood in this book. I sent Xavier an email with this request, and he liked the idea. He gave me permission to include this story in *Northern Kids*.

"Many people write, email, or call me to thank me for telling the stories of the James Bay Cree," he writes. "I feel very good about this journey and it has had a very positive effect on my own life."

Xavier's story of the lost dog that swam home becomes even more amazing when you trace the mutt's journey with your fingertip on a good map of northern Canada.

First, find the giant Hudson Bay in the middle of the map. You can't miss it. It's the second largest bay in the world, more than one thousand kilometres long, and one thousand kilometres wide. English-speaking people called it Hudson Bay because Henry Hudson, an Englishman, explored the coastline in the ship *Discovery* in 1610. The Cree people of northern Canada call the bay *Wînipekw* (in the southern dialect) or *Wînipâkw* (in the northern dialect), meaning muddy water.

Just below Hudson's Bay is the smaller James Bay. The First Nations people who live in small communities along the west coast of James Bay call themselves the Mushkegowak. Of the ten thousand people who live in their communities, children and youth make up anywhere from 50 to 60 per cent of the population.

Now find Akimiski Island, just off the west coast, and trace your finger along the Attawapiskat River to the village of Attawapiskat. You'll see how far the little dog travelled to reach his home.

Xavier Kataquapit grew up in a large family in Attawapiskat. The son of Marius and Susan Kataquapit, he had two sisters, Jackie and Janie, and five brothers, Lawrence, Mario, Antoine, Philip, Joseph, and Paul. The entire family was in the boat on the day of the story.

About fifteen hundred people live in Attawapiskat today. To go there, you have to fly in a plane or drive on an ice road in winter or travel by barge on James Bay in the summer. There are no regular highways or train links to the village, and travelling is very expensive.

"My parents were raised in a world where dogs were considered working animals dedicated to helping our people, the Cree, survive on the land," Xavier writes. "These animals were first and foremost sled dogs capable of pulling heavy loads across the snow and ice on sleds.

"In a wilderness camp, they were also useful as watchdogs that kept families aware of any dangers from wild animals. When our people were forced to give up a nomadic lifestyle on the land, the usefulness of a dog was almost lost. Still, people kept dogs around out of habit and linked to tradition.

"During my childhood, my brothers and sisters and I learned through popular culture that we could have a family dog as a pet. When I was a kid it seemed like just about everybody in Attawapiskat had a dog."

I travelled to Attawapiskat in May 2010 to write a story for *Canadian Geographic* magazine about the community's long, long struggle for a proper school. In 1979 broken pipes underneath J.R. Nakogee Elementary School began to leak toxic diesel fuel under the building, and all around the schoolyard. Worried about their children's health, Attawapiskat parents took their children out of school on May 11, 2000, when they had firm evidence of contamination. The kids never went back. Since then the school has been demolished, and the old school site has been fenced.

For more than ten years, the children of Attawapiskat have gone to school in eleven portable classrooms that are in very poor condition. The kids have no playground, swings, slides, or monkey bars—only an old fire hydrant to play on at recess. They have no soccer field or baseball field. They have no school gym, no library, no cafeteria, no art room, no music room, and no full access for wheelchairs—in fact, their school has not much of anything. Every time the kids leave their classroom to go to another class, even on the coldest days of winter blizzard, they have to pull on their winter clothes and go outside.

Inside and outside the community, many people have been demanding a new school for them.

"It is certain that if this were happening in southern Ontario, things would be very different by now," Xavier wrote in a column in 2008. "I am appalled at the way our federal government has treated the people in Attawapiskat, my home community."

The Canadian government has promised the kids of Attawapiskat a new school, year after year after year. In December 2009, the government made another promise, so I hope the school will be built by the time you read this story. Xavier Kataquapit hopes so too.

The writer makes his home in Iroquois Falls, another town in northern Ontario. You can read more of his writing in his book, *Stories of the Cree*, or on his website, www.underthenorthernsky. com. If you want to learn more about the First Nations kids who live along the western coast of James Bay, the *Wawatay News* posts stories and pictures online at www.wawataynews.ca.

Marla Kaye of Old Crow.

Up in My Bunk Bed

Marla Kaye, age nine
Cabin at Blue Bluff,
on the Porcupine River, northern Yukon, 1985

What do you do when it is too cold to step outside your door?

When a winter blizzard is swirling around your cabin, and the temperature outside the door is forty-five degrees below zero, and it's midnight dark in the late afternoon in December, what do you do for fun?

Don't tell me to watch television. We don't have a TV here.

Don't tell me to call my friends to come over. They live way up the river in Old Crow. I'm here at Blue Bluff with my two brothers and my mum and dad. We have been here at our camp for five months.

I've read all of my books and comic books many times. I've finished every bit of the schoolwork that my teacher gave me before I left school. Right now everyone in this family has something to do except me. My father is splitting firewood outside, and bringing it in for the wood stove. My two brothers are swapping hockey cards. My mother is carrying a small box to the table, and lighting another lantern so she can see clearly as she works.

What will I do?

I think I know.

■ ■ ■

First, I will climb. Whenever I want to be by myself in this cabin, I scramble up the wooden ladder to my bunk bed. When my parents built beds for us, they made my top bunk so high that it almost feels like a ledge under the ceiling. My bed is soft and comfortable, a nest of warm blankets and soft pillows just for me.

When I wake up in the morning, I can look out my window and whisper hello to a raven in the tree. Before I go to sleep, I can watch the northern lights flash across the black sky—streaks of blue, green, yellow, and orange that move back and forth like a magic wand.

My bunk bed is not just for waking up and going to sleep, and it is not just for looking out the window.

My bed is my own sky-high room. When nobody is looking, I can take a plate of warm bannock and blueberry jam up the ladder for an afternoon snack. I can curl up under a blanket and read my craft book all afternoon. I can make up stories in my head, or write things on scraps of paper that I hide under my pillow. I can watch people down below and pretend I am a spy searching for clues.

I spy with my little eye, something that is . . . blue!

Blue coffee pot on stove

Wayne Gretzky hockey card, Oilers colours, blue and orange

Dad's blue jeans

Blue beads in Mum's sewing box

My bunk bed is my workshop too. Sometimes I bring a box of coloured pencils, markers, and crayons up the ladder, along with a stack of construction paper, glue, and scissors. I can draw maps of the Porcupine River and the roads and trails around Old Crow. I can sketch our camp at Blue Bluff: the cabin, the wall tents, the high cache and the other cache, our boat in the river in summer, the woods in winter. I can draw a neat plan of the inside of our cabin: the beds, the shelf, the wood stove, and our wooden table. I can cut out a black paper raven and paste it to the high branches of a green paper spruce tree against a blue paper sky.

And when I get tired of drawing, and cutting, and pasting, I can lean over the edge of the bed and look down. I spy with my little eye, something that is . . . red!

Red-and-black checked flannel shirt, hanging on the wall hook
Gordie Howe hockey card, Detroit colours, red and white
Red flames, mixed with orange glow, inside the wood stove
Red beads in Mum's sewing box

I think I need a pair of spying binoculars up here. My eyes need help.

From my bed, I squint over the wooden railing to see what my mother is doing down at the table. I watch her spread out the soft, brown moosehide, measure it, and cut it. She strokes the soft black velvet, and measures it, and cuts it. She takes some soft white rabbit fur, and some beaver fur, and looks back and forth at each one. Which one will she pick?

Then she sets up her loom, and opens the sewing box that holds tiny coloured beads. She sifts through the beads with her fingertips, searching for just the right shade of turquoise and yellow.

Suddenly, she looks up at me.

"Marla, do you want to try today?"

Hmm. Maybe I do.

All my life I've been watching my mother make beautiful things. She can make beaded slippers, beaded baby-carrying belts, beaded mukluks, and beaded moosehide vests. She can sew stitches so tiny they are invisible. Sometimes she can look at a pair of beaded mitts and tell you whether they were made in Old

Crow or Fort McPherson or Inuvik or Fort Yukon or Aklavik, and she can tell you which lady made them, and how we're related to that lady. Just by looking at the beading design!

My mum can take a rough marten pelt and shape it into the warmest, softest fur hat for the tiniest kid. When she's finished a pair of slippers, you think you're looking at red flower petals with curling green leaves—real ones, not just beaded ones.

I know every colour in her beading box. I know what her sewing fingers can do, and what my sewing fingers can't do yet.

"When I try to make something, I stab my thumb with the sewing needle and my thread gets all tangled up," I say to her. "It never turns out right."

She smiles up at me and doesn't say anything.

"Well, I guess I should make something for us to eat, anyway," she says. She stands up and puts away her fabric and her beading loom. Turning her back to me, she begins to stir the soup on the stove.

From my bird's nest up high, I spy with my little eye that she's left her bead box on the table. It is wide open.

I look around the room. Nobody is watching. I climb down from my bunk bed, and walk slowly and quietly past my brothers and my dad to the table. I push my hand deep into the sewing box. My mother keeps stirring the soup, humming to herself with her back turned. I close my hand around some beads. As fast as a rabbit, I walk back to my corner of the room, and climb up to my getaway place.

With one hand, I empty the beads into a small cardboard box. I pull sewing scissors and strong thread out of a purple cloth bag.

Outside my window, snow covers the land with a white

blanket. Up in my hideout, my fingertips touch red, orange, yellow, green, blue, and purple beads. Now what can I make? I begin to daydream about a new project.

I spy with my little eye, a necklace that is . . . a rainbow.

What do we know for sure?

One winter day in the village of Old Crow, Yukon—the home of the Van Tat Gwich'in First Nation—I saw the most beautiful beadwork I've ever seen in my life.

I looked at the beaded baby bonnet for a long time. Trimmed with the softest white rabbit fur, with lacing ties of fine caribou hide, the hat was covered with tiny beads shaped into colourful flowers and green leaves. Beside the little hat, I saw a decorated baby belt with beautiful beads sewn to white felt in a butterfly pattern. Mothers and grandmothers use these soft belts to carry babies on their backs. This one was on display at the John Tizya Centre, a cultural centre in the heart of Old Crow.

"Who made this?" I asked the staff members. "Could I meet her?"

It turned out that Marla Charlie had created the beautiful baby belt; it took five or six months to finish. Megan Williams, the Heritage Manager for the Van Tat Gwich'in people, told me that Marla and her mother, Elizabeth Kaye, might be happy to talk to a visitor. Both are expert beadworkers.

A few days later, I met Marla at a community feast, where she was carrying her baby Shaylynn in another beaded baby belt she'd made herself.

"How old were you when you learned how to do bead work?" I asked her.

Marla, left, and Edna Kyikavichik learning how to do beadwork.
COURTESY OF CLAIR DRAGOMAN

Marla told me she started trying to string beads at age five or six years old, but she was finishing her own projects by the time she was ten. When I visited Marla and Elizabeth at home a few days later, they showed me the beaded crafts that Marla made when she was a young girl—and the amazing work they've both done since. They showed me beaded slippers, gloves, boots, mitts, fur hats, a beaded moosehide vest—even a beaded guitar strap.

Then Marla found another treasure in her belongings—a children's book that showed *her* sewing beads into moosehide at Blue Bluff when she was a small girl.

The picture book was called *Exploring Old Crow*, and it was produced by the Department of Education in Yukon Territory in

1985. It was full of pictures of Marla—picking blueberries, skiing in the snow, dancing at a Christmas concert, and sewing, sewing, sewing with her mother in her cabin.

Today Marla is thirty-four years old, with four children of her own. She told me about how she loved the family camp at Blue Bluff, about twenty-four kilometres along the Porcupine River from Old Crow. When she was a young girl, she would sometimes stay at the camp with her parents and her brothers, Robert and Edward, for up to eight months at a time. The kids would do their schoolwork in the mornings, and then be free in the afternoons to learn on the land, and explore and have fun.

Her parents also ran a wilderness camp at Blue Bluff, so Van Tat Gwich'in kids would learn more about traditional work like hunting and fishing, and traditional arts and crafts too.

"It feels so good to get away to the bush," Marla said. "It's quiet. You go with nature."

"When I was a kid, I liked to sit up on my bunk bed in my own space. I liked to work on my projects up there on cold winter days. It was hard to learn at first, but I knew I'd still be sewing when I got older. I knew I'd get better. It takes practice to become a good sewer."

Originally from Fort McPherson in the Northwest Territories, Elizabeth learned to do beadwork as a young woman. She taught Marla how to thread a needle, how to hold the needle carefully and sew the beads to moose or caribou hide. Later, she taught her daughter how to use a bead loom and follow bead patterns.

"I just showed her, and I let it go," said Elizabeth. "I left it up to her. If there was a mistake in it, I just let it be. If it wasn't per-fect, that didn't matter. She developed her own way of doing it."

Beadwork is a very important part of traditional Van Tat Gwich'in culture. "The first time you make something, you give it away as a gift," Elizabeth explained. "It inspires you to become a better sewer."

Marla started with small projects. First, she made bead necklaces. Then she sewed tiny doll-size slippers and mitts out of moosehide, and added a little bit of beading. Later on she made her own beading loom out of a wooden stick. High in her bunk bed, she worked on many beading projects and read many craft books before she began to create her own patterns.

At her daycare centre in Old Crow, Elizabeth teaches small children how to sew. She won the Prime Minister's Award for Excellence in Early Childhood Education in 2002. "Beadwork develops eye and hand coordination," she said. "And the kids are so proud of what they make."

Marla takes her own children to the cabin at Blue Bluff, where she still likes to work on her beading projects. "Beadwork teaches you patience," she said. "It gives you your own ideas about design and colour."

To write this story, I used my imagination to picture the artistic young girl working on her craft projects high in her bunk bed. Marla checked the story, and also drew a map of the camp and an outline of the cabin for me so I could see Blue Bluff in my mind. We are both grateful to Michele Royle of the Yukon Department of Education for finding extra copies of the out-of-print picture book for Marla's children, and to Clair Dragoman for allowing his photographs to be used again in *Northern Kids*.

I have used the modern spelling when I refer to the Van Tat Gwich'in, but you will find other spellings, including Vuntut

Gwitchin, the name of the local government. It means "people of the lakes," and it refers to their larger traditional territory. To learn more about the Van Tat Gwich'in First Nation online, you can explore the website www.oldcrow.ca. The community has also recently completed a beautiful book about its history and culture, based on elders' stories, called *People of the Lakes*. The best way to learn about the Yukon's most northern community is to go north for a visit—and see Marla's and Elizabeth's beadwork for yourself.

Too' Oh Zrii and the Bear

Tammy Josie, age eight
Camp in Driftwood River, Yukon, 1991

I always like going upriver with my family every year. We stay near Driftwood River, about fifty-seven kilometres up Porcupine River from Old Crow. I remember this one time we were staying in a wall tent: my dad William, my mom Vicky, my Uncle Alvie, my brother Paul, and me, all sleeping on caribou skin mattresses. We had a dog named Too' Oh Zrii—you pronounce it Toe-oh-zree, and it means "the moon." He had the mark of a crescent moon on his forehead.

As we were sleeping one night, we had a visitor from the bushes beyond.

My uncle got up first when he heard the dog whimpering. And then he heard a loud, heavy breathing, grunting noise. He woke up my father, William, who had the gun beside him. The men stayed at either side of the tent walls keeping my mother, brother and me safe from whatever was outside, curious about what we were.

As soon as Too' Oh Zrii noticed that people were up, he stood and started growling. He could act tough now that gun was around! My father didn't bother waking up my mother or us kids so that we wouldn't startle the bear in his own domain. The next day, my father and uncle told me that they had stayed perfectly still and waited the bear out. They knew the bear was just curious to see something foreign in his territory . . .

In the morning, we woke up around five or six o'clock—as that is when caribou or moose cross rivers—to find a dirty bear paw print on the outer door of our tent.

Tammy Josie and her grandmother, the late
Miss Edith Josie, near Old Crow, Yukon.

He wanted us to know that he was there, that he wasn't afraid of us, and that we were on his land.

We still camp at that spot, but we also understand that we live in bear country, and he gets his respect.

Trapline Jitters

One time when I was a bit younger, my grandmother, Miss Edith Josie, came home with snare wire.

I guess she wanted to teach me how to trap and make a living like the old ways, how she was raised. We sat together in front of the wood stove, as that is where we always sat when she was showing me something, and we made the snares ready to go.

The next day, we went out and she showed me how to set rabbit snares in thick willow, and we made a little trapline. I thought this was the coolest thing. I would be having fried rabbit every day! We went to check our trapline early the next day. We found a dead rabbit in the snare, frozen. My grandmother showed me how to take it out of the snare, how to reset the snare, and how to make sure not to leave a scent behind. I would then put the rabbit on the sleigh, and we would continue on our trails.

After I got the hang of it, we came across a live rabbit in a snare.

"Let's walk the rest of the line and come back to it later," I tried to tell my Gramma. I was thinking that it would be frozen later, and then I could take it out of the trap. She looked mad at me and told me to grab that rabbit and twist its neck.

I didn't want to do this. Gramma looked even more mad, and she grabbed that rabbit, twisted its neck, and snapped the spine. It screamed a sound that frightened me, and I started to cry. Gramma looked really mad now. She grabbed my hand and made me carry that rabbit the rest of the way home. When we got back to her place, she made me tear the skin off the rabbit and cook it. Then, I had to eat it.

We took down the snares that night and we haven't gone on any trapping expeditions since that day. I don't blame her.

What do we know for sure?

Tammy Josie is a writer and storyteller from the Van Tat Gwich'in First Nation in Old Crow, Yukon. I met her at a sad time in her life. Her grandmother, Miss Edith Josie—a famous Canadian writer I had respected for a long time—had died just two days earlier, at the age of eighty-eight. People in Old Crow stopped all of their ordinary activities to prepare for the funeral and burial and to welcome visitors from across the north to honour this well-loved elder at a community feast.

Tammy spoke at the funeral about the privilege of growing up with her grandmother. When she told the story of the rabbit-snaring lesson, everyone laughed. Northerners understand that kids can be a bit scared of trapping at first. Grandparents need to teach young children that their food comes from the land, and that hunting and trapping—and living and dying—are a part of the natural cycle of life. Maybe Tammy's grandmother was also trying to teach her that a trapped animal should die quickly, not slowly.

Miss Edith Josie was a very kind woman who wrote a newspaper column, "Here Are The News," for more than forty years. Her stories about the daily lives and traditions of the Van Tat Gwich'in people of Old Crow appeared in the *Whitehorse Star* and in many other Canadian newspapers, and then travelled around the world in German, Italian, Finnish, and Spanish translations. The writer was awarded the Order of Canada, the Centennial Medal, and many other honours for her contributions to the cultural life of our country. And yet she lived her whole life in a small village, and out on the land she loved so much.

Perhaps it's natural that Tammy grew up to love stories too. As a teenager and young woman, she appeared at storytelling festivals with her grandmother. She also helped with a special project to interview Van Tat Gwich'in elders about their traditional knowledge. When her grandmother became ill in 2009, Tammy came home to Old Crow to take care of her.

Tammy wants to carry on Edith Josie's storytelling tradition in the future. Right now, she lives in Whitehorse.

Erin Browne and her horse, Snoopy, riding
with her brother Jeremy and his horse, Jake.
COURTESY OF BROWNE FAMILY COLLECTION

Snoopy

Erin Browne, age sixteen
Tetsa River, BC, 2005

If I ever had doubts about Snoopy, they've disappeared for good. She proved herself last night—and gave me courage when I'd lost mine.

Snoopy is the first horse I've ever trained on my own, and I'm her first rider. She's a paint, and if you don't know your horse breeds, just think about a mare with rusty brown and white markings on her. A little beauty. She's just three years old, with a crazy spirit that keeps me laughing.

Snoopy had the biggest conniption the first time I tried to ride her across a river. No way was she going to carry me, and she let me know it. I couldn't even get her to move at all, so my brother Jeremy tried to urge her across the water. She reared, threw him off, and ran home. It was pretty hilarious to watch him stomp home, covered in mud. Now Snoopy loves the water so much she stops right in the middle of the current and won't budge. Like she's found her own personal Jacuzzi, or something.

"C'mon, Snoopy, let's get a move on!" I say. "Let's go!"

Snoopy pretends she doesn't hear me. She stands in the river, cooling off her belly, soaking her small hooves likes she needs a pedicure, daring me to jump into the water myself. She is teaching me as much about stubborn horses as I'm teaching her about stubborn humans.

I guess I had it easy with my first horse, Spooky. Talking breeds again, he's a Morgan, and they're bred for cart racing, but you won't see Spooky galloping much anymore. Would you believe he's thirty-nine years old? That's ancient for a horse. We've known each other all my life, and by now he can read my mind like a book. I don't even need to nudge him on the trail. Just a little whisper, and he knows where to go.

Spooky won't be with us much longer. I realize that. I know it will be hard for me to face the death of a best friend. That's part of the reason I got Snoopy this year. She'll be here with me on the day that Spooky dies, and I think her sense of humour might be a big comfort to me.

We've always had about thirty horses around our place. My dad transports hunters and other travellers into the mountains on horseback and camps out with them in the bush. That's our family business. Visitors usually come in the fall, so we try to go out on our own family hunting trips just before they arrive.

On Friday, we left the house for the mountains. We expected to be away from home for about a week, so it took a bit of time to get our camping gear together. We decided to take six horses with us. Mom and Dad would each ride their own horses, and they'd lead two other pack horses. Jeremy would ride his horse, Hairy. I'd ride Snoopy and carry along our new puppy, Spike, an adorable red heeler.

As I threw the saddle on Snoopy, I had my doubts about how this silly mare was going to manage an elk-hunting trip in unfamiliar territory. I shouldn't have worried. That horse proved her strength on one terrifying night.

■ ■ ■

We set out on the trail a little late in the day. The four of us rode through the trees and up into the hills. In our country, the poplar leaves turn golden in early fall, under a brilliant blue sky, so it was a beautiful ride. We arrived in the dark at what my dad calls High Camp, unsaddled and tethered four of the horses to let them eat, and then set up our tents and beds.

Jeremy and I trudged down to the creek about a kilometre away with the two pack horses and filled the pack boxes with water for the horses. After every horse had a drink, we unsaddled and tethered our pack horses and went happily into our bedrolls. Sleeping in the bush is a great experience, because all you can hear is the rush of the wind around you—and the horse bells. We put bells around the horses' necks so we don't lose them.

Early in the morning, around six o'clock, we saddled up our riding horses and the two pack horses with empty packs that we hoped would soon be full of elk meat. Then we rode up into the mountains to begin our search for elk.

Have you seen elk? They're the largest members of the deer family, and not easy to hunt. We thought we'd need at least a week to find one for our freezer this winter, but we got lucky on the first day. We found a good place to watch for big animals— way high up with a good view of the valley—and then we pulled our binoculars out of our packs. Late afternoon turned to early evening. We waited.

Suddenly . . .

"There! Look!"

Mom was the first to spot the elk. She followed the animal with her binoculars, and then she picked up her hunting rifle. She raised it to her shoulder and aimed carefully.

My mother is an excellent hunter, which sometimes surprises me because she didn't learn how to shoot when she was a kid, the way Jeremy and I did. She was born in Nova Scotia and came up here as a Katimavik volunteer to help build an ice rink in Toad River. Like a lot of people from away—as she calls newcomers— she never planned to stay, but she met my dad. She fell for the man and the north at the same time. He taught her how to enjoy life in this part of Canada, and how to hunt.

I heard the sharp shot of Mom's rifle. I covered our new puppy's ears with my hands so the sound wouldn't scare him.

"I think I got it," Mom said. We all stared through our binoculars, but couldn't see the animal anymore. The sun was beginning to set, and my dad turned to Jeremy and me.

"It will be dark soon," he told us. "Your mom and I will need some time to find the elk in the bush, and we might not find it in this light. The horses badly need some water. Do you think you can take them back to the creek to drink, and then come back? It looks like we might be camping up here for the night."

That sounded like a smart idea. Jeremy and I guided our parents' horses, and the two pack horses, and we rode back down to the trail. Jeremy led the way on Hairy, and I followed on Snoopy, hoping my young rebel would behave herself when we reached the creek.

We enjoyed the first part of the ride, stopping to look at things here and there. Jeremy and I have been exploring these trails together ever since we learned how to ride. Sometimes we go on hunting trips, just the two of us. In the winter, we also run a short trapline of about five kilometres through the woods. After school, we dump our textbooks on the kitchen table and pull on heavy winter parkas, snow pants, and high winter boots to go out and check our traps. Last year we caught one hundred and seventeen squirrels, eight lynx, two wolves and a wolverine. We unload the traps, put our catch in our backpacks, and go home to thaw out the carcasses, skin the animals, and stretch them. Then we bundle up the pelts and send them to Western Canadian Fur Auction. Soon enough, the cheques come back, two dollars a squirrel this year. Our highest-selling lynx brought back four hundred dollars at auction. You could say that's *our* family business, but it's for the winter ahead. Early fall is for elk hunting.

"Which trail should we take to the creek?" Jeremy asked me over his shoulder.

I looked around. Now that we were in deep forest, the darkness was coming on a little too early for my liking. I wasn't sure I could even see the trail anymore.

"Oh, just the usual way," I answered. "You know."

So far Snoopy seemed willing to walk along without stopping for a little munch of the tall grass in the woods. Jeremy's horse pushed through the undergrowth, making a path for us to follow.

It took a lot longer to reach the creek than we expected. By the time we found the stream, all six horses looked thirsty enough to drink the entire Tetsa River. Snoopy bolted ahead of the older horses to take the first sip.

As we waited, Jeremy and I looked around. It was night.

■　■　■

"How are we going to get back?" I asked my brother.

"Same way we came," he answered with his usual confidence.

I wondered whether my brother felt as brave as he sounded. We organized the horses, and set off through the bush again to return to our parents. Jeremy held a flashlight up above his head to try to find the twisting, turning trail. Once it gets dark in the woods, do you think it's possible for it to get darker? Clouds drifted across the moon. Stars couldn't twinkle brightly enough to help that flashlight. We squinted into the darkness, trying to find our way.

"What was that noise?" My voice came out as a squeak. Jeremy turned around to listen.

My heart pounded as I listened to the low snorting, snuffling noise of an unknown animal. Could it be a bear, searching for a cub on the other side of our path? Would she see us as her enemies? Suddenly the bush came alive with scary night noises. An owl's hoot sent a shiver up my backbone. I could feel my hands trembling on Snoopy's reins as I leaned forward to peer into the woods. What was out there, waiting for us? Swooping bats? A pack of wolves? That angry mama bear, furious with the intruders?

When a low branch slapped me across the face and snapped off, I yelled in surprise. Snoopy reared back, but she didn't throw me off her back or bolt into the trees. I realized that my crazy little horse was calmer than me.

We kept riding. "Are we lost?" I asked Jeremy.

My brother just looked at me. I'd seen that same look on Jeremy's face many days on our trapline, like when we had a trapped wolverine snarling at us and it was minus thirty-five degrees outside, and one of us had take off our darns mitts and deal with the situation. With that look of his, I always knew what Jeremy was trying to tell me: *Nobody is here but us. We have to figure out this problem on our own.*

Right. I peered into the darkness and nudged Snoopy forward.

"It must be very late, so we have to keep riding," I told my brother. He nodded and held his flashlight high so I could see it. We didn't know where we were going—but we just kept going.

Speaking softly to our horses, we guided them around rocks and boulders, through tangled underbrush and creek beds, over fallen logs and stumps.

Jeremy and I were hungry by this time, fiercely hungry. I realized that we hadn't eaten since just after noon, when we'd munched a bit of trail mix. By now it must be at least ten or eleven o'clock. The night air was cold and damp, and the wind hit us in the face. I wasn't trembling anymore. I was shaking. What if we'd travelled beyond the reach of the trails our parents knew? What if that bear were following us, searching for a midnight snack of her own?

Leaning over, I began to stroke Snoopy's mane. She wasn't terrified. She was a lot lower to the ground than me, pushing through the poking, scratching branches, and yet she put one hoof in front of the other without hesitation. I was so sleepy that I was ready to tumble off the saddle, but I was too scared to close my eyes. Snoopy had no fear. I reached forward and put the palms of my hands on her warm neck. Slowly her warmth calmed me down.

At last I heard a happy shout from my brother. "I see a little speck of fire. I think it's their campfire!"

We began to shout ahead to our parents, and they shouted back to us so we could find our way. We climbed the final hill, jumped off our horses, and ran towards them. What a relief! Two kids, two parents, six horses, and a puppy couldn't stop grinning at each other. My dad gave us an orange from his saddlebag, a bottle of drinking water, and then we speared some fresh elk meat on sticks to roast over the campfire. I don't think I've ever tasted anything so delicious in my life.

As I was falling asleep under the tarp, warm under a heavy horse blanket, with Spike snoring near my head, I heard the soft whinny of a proud, young horse. She'd taught me a thing or two in those woods, and she knew it.

Thanks, Snoopy. You're my friend forever.

What do we know for sure?

I'd like to thank the kids of Toad River, BC, for bringing this story to me.

I stopped in Toad River—population, about fifty depending on the day—while I was travelling north to the Yukon. Toad River is at Mile 422 on the Alaska Highway, which I prefer to call the AlCan Highway because the road meanders a long distance inside Canada too.

The tiny community is a bit hard to find on the map. If you look hard enough, you'll find it north of Fort Nelson, just inside the Muskwa-Kechika Management Area. This is a huge wilderness of mountains, forests, and rivers that covers 6.4 million hectares of northern British Columbia—an area roughly the same size as Ireland. The traditional territory of the Kaska Dena, Treaty 8 and Carrier-Sekani First Nations has been a special protected area since 1998. Oil and gas exploration, hunting, and fishing are allowed, but are watched carefully under strict rules so that the wilderness will not be damaged by over-development.

On my first day in Toad River, I watched three moose swim across a lake behind my cabin. On the second day, I visited the world-famous hat collection in the Toad River Lodge café. More than sixty-eight hundred truckers' caps are nailed to the ceiling. Try concentrating on eating a world-famous salmon burger while also counting hats from all over North America.

On my third day in Toad River, I visited the kids in one of the smallest schools in Canada. In 2009 Toad River School had twelve students from kindergarten to Grade 12. Through the years, students have travelled to the two-room school by snowmobile, horseback, on foot, and even on the small planes that can land on the airstrip beside the playground.

After my visit, I wrote about the friendly kids of Toad River on my blog. A few months later, I received an email from Erin Browne, a fourth-year psychology student at the University of Northern British Columbia in Prince George. She had attended Toad River School from kindergarten through Grade 12, and it turned out that she was preparing a presentation for one of her university courses about her home community. Would I like to read it? I sure would.

I learned that a fur-trading post opened on the same site in 1867, but it closed about twenty years later, probably due to its isolation.

It is much too cold for toads to live in Toad River. You won't find a lot of leaping amphibians in this part of the woods. The story goes that the village owes its odd name to the American soldiers who were building the famous highway through the area during the Second World War. There was no bridge across the Racing River, so their supplies had to be "towed" across. So maybe some mapmaker forgot how to spell. A highway maintenance camp sprang up on the site in 1942, and that's what Toad River has been ever since.

Many children in Toad River come from the hard-working families who keep the wilderness highway open through the mountains in every kind of weather. Other families work in the tourism business, usually with visiting hunters.

Erin's family lives about an hour down the highway from Toad River. Her parents run Steamboat Mountain Outfitters. They built their own log home near the Tetsa River, and heated it with a wood-burning furnace and wood stove. When Erin was little, the Brownes collected water from a creek behind the house, and lit their home with propane light. They had no electricity or running water. These days, they have a battery-operated generator for the water pump and lights, and a generator to run the washing machine, TV, and computer. The family has dial-up Internet too.

To go to Toad River School, Erin and Jeremy had to get up with their mother early in the morning to feed the horses and dogs, then drive an hour on the highway to school. The kids attended classes for just four days a week due to the distance of daily travelling, so they always had a long weekend. This allowed them time to do lots of hunting, trapping, camping, and exploring on horseback.

When I asked Erin to share one of her favourite stories with me, she told me three of them—about a baby moose that got caught in a barbed wire fence, and then chased her all over her yard; about an angry wolverine on her trapline; and about the time she and Jeremy had an adventure on an elk hunting trip. I wrote the last story, and Erin checked it and added more details.

Her wonderful first horse, Spooky, died in 2006 at the age of forty. Snoopy—the brave and spirited paint—is seven years old, still exploring the wilderness of northern BC. Jeremy is now a carpenter in Dawson Creek. Erin hopes to become a clinical neuropsychologist, a career that will probably require that she live in a city. Someday she hopes to return to the north to live.

"I didn't realize that northern kids had a different way of life until I moved away," she told me. "The biggest difference is that you have an opportunity to prove to yourself that you can do anything."

Breanna Lancaster, preparing the moose meat.

Moose Camp

Breanna Lancaster, age ten
Dawson City, Yukon, 2009

I live in Dredge Pond, near Dawson City. It is a cool place where miners look for gold. I like it because there aren't a bunch of cars, zooming up and down. We have lot of ponds, rivers, and creeks to explore near our place. I live with my mum and dad and my younger brother, Caden, in a house my parents built.

This fall I had a chance to go to moose camp. You are supposed to be eleven years old and older; I was only a year too young, so they said I could go. I didn't want to wait a whole year. If you want to go to moose camp, you go to the Tr'ondëk Hwëch'in community hall, and you fill out a form.

Moose camp goes from Thursday to Sunday. It happens in September. This year six girls and three boys climbed into a car and trucks, along with the grown-up camp leaders. We drove all the way to Blackstone Camp, about two and a half hours up the Dempster Highway into the mountains. The Tr'ondëk Hwëch'in have a special camp there with buildings where you can eat and sleep. When we got there, it was already dark. We ran into the building, carrying all of our stuff for camp.

"I want the top bunk!" I shouted.

Everybody shouted the same thing. I guess camp is always like that.

After a while, we settled down and went to sleep. In the morning we got up early, around seven thirty or eight o'clock. Inside, it was warm beside the wood stove, but it was pretty cold outside. There was no snow yet in Dawson, but up here, the first snow had already come. So we had to dress right. I wore two sweaters with long sleeves on top of each other, snow pants, a winter jacket, a tuque, big woolly socks, and black winter boots. I also brought rubber boots and another rain jacket. We had to bring extra clothes in case some got wet, because we were outside most of the time.

We ate a big breakfast. Right away we went out moose hunting.

We learned everything about the moose: how it lives, how to follow it, how to hunt it. We learned about moose calls. We didn't find any animals ourselves, but grown-up hunters went away in a truck and a four-wheeler to look for them too.

We hiked on the land through the day, exploring things. The camp leaders showed us lots of medicine plants we hadn't seen before. We saw some mountain sheep. When we went back to camp, we ate tinned salmon and bannock for our lunch, played games outside, and awesome things like that. We interviewed Jackie about how the climate is changing across the north, more than many other places, and how it is affecting the animals and the people. We played bingo too. They had lots of treats for us to eat.

The camp had an eating place and kitchen cabin, and there were separate sleeping places. The girls were not allowed to go to the boys' place, and the boys were not allowed to come to our place. We sat on our beds and talked until very late.

Around midnight, we heard the hunters' truck come back. We jumped down off the bunk beds and ran outside, shining flashlights.

Everybody asked the same question. I guess moose camp is always like that.

"Look for yourself," said one of the leaders. I shone my flashlight at the back of the truck: they had brought back two dead moose.

Hunting doesn't scare me, and it doesn't bother me. My parents hunt too. We have caribou meat in our freezer right now. Me and my dad and my friend Tiffany snared and skinned a rabbit together at home. It's food. You have to eat.

I love all animals. You wouldn't kill them all or they would become extinct. We learned this at moose camp: *Take only what you need. Use all that you take.*

The next day, we learned how to cut up the moose into large pieces and pack it home in the truck. The hunters cut the four quarters of the animal. They cut off the head.

"Never say *eeew* or *gross* or *yuck* or words like that," a camp leader told us later on. "It's your food you are handling, good food for yourself or your family or an elder in Dawson. You have to respect it. Good hunters say that if you make fun of your food, you will have bad luck on your next hunt."

Funny birds flew around us as we looked at the moose. These birds are called whiskeyjacks, or sometimes, camp robbers. Maybe they wanted some meat too, or maybe they just wanted to watch what was happening. As the grown-ups showed us how to butcher the moose, they told us what we would do next. When we got back to town, they said, we had to help with our own hands as much as we could.

On the last day of moose camp, the hunters brought the two moose back to town in their truck. We went home too. Then the moose meat had to hang in sheds for four to five days to be ready for the next step in our work.

We waited and waited. Finally, I walked with a whole bunch of kids from our school over to the Tr'ondëk Hwëch'in hall, to the kitchen part, to cut up the moose meat into smaller pieces

Moose Camp, 2009. Breanna is in the striped shirt, carrying a coat.

and pack it into freezer bags. The camp leaders told us again about how to respect our food as we cut it up. We put all the meat in bags to share with the community. When we were finished, everybody in town came for a big feast at the hall. Before people left, we handed out the bags of moose meat.

We gave the meat to the elders first. They smiled at us, and I could tell they were happy that we were moose hunters too.

I brought my own moose meat home too. All year people in

Dawson will be eating mooseburgers, moose stew, roast moose, and moose soup. My favourite is moose ribs. Delicious!

What do we know for sure?

You might remember Breanna Lancaster, the historical detective who researched the story about the terrible house fire in Dawson City in 1917. You'll find that story on page 44.

When I visited her at her home to learn more about her great-great aunt's family and the fire, Breanna told me about her own adventures at moose camp. She hopes to go back again this year because she enjoyed it so much. I had extra questions, so I went to visit Georgette McLeod, who is the traditional knowledge specialist for the Tr'ondëk Hwëch'in First Nation.

Every year the Tr'ondëk Hwëch'in invite kids in the community to learn more about moose hunting at a fall camp in the Blackstone Uplands, a beautiful area along Canada's most northern highway—the Dempster Highway—between Dawson and Inuvik. The First Nation also organizes First Hunt and First Fish—two special events that teach kids about traditional caribou hunting and fishing methods.

Kids have a lot of fun at moose-hunting camp too. The elders in the community are happy to see a new generation enjoy hunting for food.

"In the past, the tradition was that only men and boys would go moose hunting, while the girls had other responsibilities later, such as preparing the meat and tanning the hides," Georgette explained.

"The elders taught boys to give away the first animal they harvested to people in the community," she said. The Tr'ondëk

Hwëch'in believed this gift would bring good luck to the young hunters as they searched for animals in the future, but they also wanted to teach the importance of sharing.

"Now we encourage girls to go hunting too," Georgette said. The moose hunting camp and the fish camp are open to any kids in the community, including kids like Breanna who are not members of the Tr'ondëk Hwëch'in First Nation.

In the story, Breanna mentions that the kids interviewed a woman named Jackie about climate change in the north. Jackie Olson is the heritage director for the Tr'ondëk Hwëch'in, and like many northerners, she is very concerned about how the warmer temperatures, melting glaciers, and melting permafrost will affect the people and animals in the northern Yukon, including the moose. To learn more about climate change in northern Canada, visit www.climatechangenorth.ca.

Scientists estimate that Canada is home to between five hundred thousand and one million moose. The moose is the largest member of the deer family. These powerful forest animals have strong bodies, long noses, and tall, skinny legs. Although they have very poor eyesight, they are excellent swimmers, and can dive more than five metres into deep, northern lakes. They are also known for their wide antlers, which they shed in the fall. Some northern Canadians make interesting crafts out of these shed antlers—in fact, I once saw a full chandelier in Wanyandie Flats, Alberta, made out of moose antlers. People also decorate the outside of their houses with them.

As Breanna said, every part of the harvested moose is used for something. Experienced elders know how to scrape, dry, and tan the moose hide until it feels like the softest leather. They make these hides into beaded slippers, sometimes called moccasins, as well as mukluks, gloves, traditional clothing for special occasions, and many different crafts. In the old days, northerners also made moose-skin boats.

Moose hunting remains an important part of life in the north. A bull moose can weigh up to six hundred kilograms and be more than two metres high, large enough to provide a good supply of meat for several families for a year. To learn more about these important animals, check the Hinterland Who's Who website at www.hww.ca.

Francis Bouffard of West Dawson, Yukon, is one of the twelve hundred
Junior Canadian Rangers in Canada's three northern territories.

True North Spirit

Francis Bouffard, age fourteen
West Dawson, Yukon, 2010

When I'm out in the bush, I feel free. I can go anywhere, exploring. I've lived in Whitehorse before, and I don't really like it. All the people, all the crowded places, all the traffic. It's not for me. This place is better for me.

I was born at 100 Mile House in northern British Columbia, but I've lived in the Yukon for as long as I can remember. When I was little, we had a cabin in the bush not too far from Whitehorse, down Long Lake Road. My first memories are about snow—the first snowfall of the year came down but melted in less than five hours. Next day, it snowed again and we made snowmen and snow angels. We could only make snowmen at the beginning and end of the winter—the rest of the time it was too cold. I remember my two brothers and me climbing trees, getting lost in the woods and finding our way back, grouse hunting, berry picking, huge spring mud puddles.

My dad was a trapper. My mum and two brothers, Emile and Galen, and me—we were all into that life too. We had dogs—Fare, Zig, Freda, and Russ. When we were little, Mum would pack us into the dogsled for a ride. Sometimes she would spend an hour trying to harness the dogs the right way. Just as we were ready to take off, the dogs would get away without her. Off we went flying down the trail, with her running after us, hollering. The sled hit a tree before too long, but no one got hurt.

Our family lived in a wood-frame cabin with a big garden and a shop—a separate building where we butchered the meat. For electricity, we had solar panels that charged several batteries, and sometimes we'd use a generator when there wasn't enough light. We didn't have a refrigerator; we had a cold room. In the cold room there was a small square hole that we could open and close to let cold air in. In the summer, we had a hole in the ground in the shade to keep eggs and milk.

In those days, my dad also cut wood and sold it to people in town. He would cut the trees, Mom would limb the branches, and me and my brothers would move the brush out of the way. We also helped to stack the wood and bring it into the house. We heated our house with a wood stove back then, and we still do.

We got our water from a creek before the beavers moved in, and after that we got water from town. We had a big tank in the back of our truck that we would fill up, and then pump into the tank in our house. These days we still haul our water from town in blue jugs, but we use melted snow and rainwater for washing. There is always a lot of work to do, but that's okay. Our family had this great, old truck we called Mighty Blue. It got that name because one day Mom accidentally drove the truck the wrong way onto a road that hadn't been used all winter. The snow was deep. We were stuck for a while, but the Mighty Blue worked its way out and earned its name. We were all glad, because we were just heading out to the high camp for our spring visit.

Television? Well, we had a TV set that ran off the generator, but we only watched videos on it. No television shows. It's about the same today, but we watch movies on a laptop. In Grade 1 we started going to Whitehorse every day to go to school. Mom or Dad used to drive us in. Later on, we lived in the city for a short while—didn't like it. We moved to Dawson when I was in Grade 3.

I've lived around here ever since. This place seems about right for me. We live in West Dawson now. It's on the far side of the Yukon River from the town. To get to our cabin, we take a ferry or our canoe or motorboat across the river in the summer months. In winter, we walk or skidoo across the ice bridge. For maybe three weeks in the spring and fall—when the ice is breaking up, the winter road is gone, and the ferry can't run—we are cut off from town. We either stock up on enough food to get us through or we move to town for the time. We don't really miss anything—except one time when we watched, through the binoculars, as the ice cream store first reopened and gave away free ice cream all day long to the locals.

Early this winter, one of our neighbours tried to do a favour for everybody in West Dawson by plowing the ice road early in the winter. The ice wasn't strong enough. His pick-up truck plunged through the ice, head first, and froze solid with its tailgate up in the air. The driver wasn't hurt, luckily. It took weeks to get that truck free, and we all walked out on the ice to have a good laugh at it.

Our cabin is a log house, up on top of a hill. There are three rooms: two big ones downstairs, and one upstairs, with a steep stairway. We have two wood stoves in the house, and a big wide porch at the front. We are surrounded by trees, and it's nice and quiet. We have friendly neighbours a short walk away, but everybody has their privacy.

School is about two kilometres away, and it doesn't take us very long to walk there. Since we live at the top of a hill, in the winter we can toboggan from the house straight down to the river—cuts down on the travel time. When I come home in the afternoon, I pull the toboggan up the hill to the starting place, ready for the next day.

Winter is definitely my favourite season, because there are lots more things to do that I like. It can get cold here—down to minus forty or minus fifty—but we don't make a big deal of it. Everybody in Dawson knows how to dress for winter. We have the gear we need, and we know what to do to stay comfortable when we're outside. It is dark, but the pay-off is that we get almost twenty-four hours of daylight in summer, and long, warm days for biking, exploring, hiking, fishing, camping and all of that. I am saving my money for a skidoo of my own and also a dirt bike.

I joined the Junior Canadian Rangers in 2006 for a lot of reasons, and I'm really glad I did. You don't have to want to join the Canadian Rangers, or the Canadian military, to belong to it. I like it because of all the trips we get to go on, and how we can learn more bush and survival skills. We've learned gun, ATV, and skidoo safety, and we're starting to learn about skidoo and small engine maintenance and repairs.

I really enjoyed the chance to go to Whitehorse for ETS—Enhanced Training Session—and I met a bunch of Junior Rangers from different communities all over the north, including the Northwest Territories and Nunavut. We did things like swimming, rock climbing and zip line, target shooting, horseback riding, whitewater rafting, and canoeing. I did pretty well in a shooting competition—got first place of everyone there.

I've always liked hunting. I've gone on the First Hunt with the Tr'ondëk Hwëch'in for the last few years, where we learn to hunt for caribou, mountain sheep, birds, grouse, ptarmigan, and rabbits. I like the adventure of the hunt, following the animals, and watching what they do. We've learned how to butcher the animal, how to skin and dry the meat, and I've been trying to improve my shooting and hunting skills. I like helping out in the community, and providing meat for the elders who can't hunt anymore.

We go to fish camp in the spring for salmon—king and chum—and I also have learned how to use gill nets and snares and traps.

I am thinking about going into the Canadian Rangers when I get older. They do important work in Search and Rescue. If someone is lost in the bush, or trapped on the river somehow, the Rangers are the ones who know how to look for them. I think I'll always want to live in the north. That's just who I am.

What do we know for sure?

One day when I was living in Dawson City, I met a friendly woman named Freda Roberts, who takes kids on the Tr'ondëk Hwëch'in First Hunt. She suggested I interview Francis Bouffard because he's become a good hunter and a responsible gun user.

I asked Francis to share his life story with me because I wanted to learn more about an independent kid who enjoys off-grid living in the Yukon—meaning life in the bush, without electricity or other city services. I also wanted to know more about the Junior Canadian Rangers.

As we ate pizza, Francis patiently answered all of my questions. Later, he checked the story for accuracy and sent me his corrections. He was fourteen years old at the time of our conversation. His brother Emile is a year and a half older than him, and his brother Galen is a year and a half younger.

Francis describes a wonderful way of life—but it's a rare one, even in the north.

The Yukon is a massive wilderness with only thirty-four thousand citizens altogether, but twenty-five thousand of them live in Whitehorse. Most other Yukoners live in seven small communities. Even in small towns, northerners can rely on most of the services that southern Canadians take for granted: schools, health clinics, paved highways, airports, public libraries, and of course, electricity and running water. Whitehorse also has the main hospital, a college, many stores, a big public library, beautiful art galleries, museums, and recreation centres. Like most Yukon kids, Francis uses the Internet, cell phones, video games, and iPods, but he has different wilderness opportunities too, and he likes them.

The Yukoners who live off-grid—like Francis and his family—choose that way of life because they enjoy living on the land in a natural way.

And what are Canadian Rangers? Well, they have an interesting story too. During the Second World War, the Canadian government worried that Japan might attack the northwest coast of BC and the Yukon. The country needed northerners to watch out for danger, and defend its territory if necessary—and so it organized the Canadian Rangers. Do you remember the story of J.J. Van Bibber and his adventurous raft trip with his brothers and sisters earlier in this book? J.J. was one of the very first Rangers.

Today the Canadian Rangers are a volunteer force of Inuit, First Nations, Metis, and non-Aboriginal northerners who work as part-time soldiers in remote, isolated, and coastal communities of Canada. They do no police work, and no fighting, of course.

Their job is to watch the northern coastline to protect Canada's Arctic sovereignty—meaning, our ownership of our northern land—and to help out in emergencies such as northern plane crashes, forest fires, or boating accidents.

Junior Canadian Rangers are not a part of the military, and they are not cadets. This is an activity program for boys and girls between the ages of twelve and eighteen who live in isolated, remote, or rural communities across Canada. The Department of National Defence and other Canadian organizations sponsor the program. About twelve hundred of the thirty-four hundred kids in the program live in Nunavut, the Yukon, and the Northwest Territories. They belong to more than one hundred and ten patrols.

Junior Rangers learn traditional northern skills such as hunting and fishing, how to make shelters in the bush, and how to live on the land. In talks with elders, they learn about their community traditions and customs, spirituality, language, music, and art. They also learn Canadian Ranger skills such as how to use small boats, snowmobiles, and all-terrain vehicles; how to use rifles safely; how to offer first aid to injured people; and how to be community leaders and volunteers. Finally, they learn life skills, including how to protect the environment and live in a healthy way. The program is free, and it offers many northern kids their first chance to travel outside their home community.

If you're travelling in the north, you'll recognize Junior Canadian Rangers by their green sweatshirts and ball caps with the maple leaf crest. You can learn more about the group at www.rangers.dnd.ca.

Devon Allooloo on one of his early caribou hunts.

The Caribou Hunter

Devon Allooloo, age fourteen
Yellowknife, Northwest Territories, 2010

I went caribou hunting for the first time when I was six years old. Probably a lot of parents wouldn't let their kids near a rifle, but my parents knew I'd be a hunter when I grew up and wanted to show me how to do it properly. When I was young, the bedtime stories told to me by my mom were about hunting—mostly about a young boy who had many adventures before bringing meat back to his family.

Ever since I was young, I wanted to be a hunter like my dad one day. My dad has been hunting since he was about six years old as well. He owned his own dog team when he was ten years old. I have a dog team now too. I've always gone out on the land with my family. We hunt for the wild meat that we eat. (Here we call it country food.) I also help my dad as a guide with sports hunters who come to the north to hunt for caribou, wolves, wolverines, polar bears, and seals. We take visitors out fishing too, for trout, grayling, northern pike, and whitefish.

I've travelled a lot across the Northwest Territories and Nunavut, to places like Thonokied Lake, White Wolf Lake, Little Marten Lake, Pellat Lake, even as far as Iqaluit and Pond Inlet, where my dad is from.

For most of my life, I haven't gone to a regular school. I like home-schooling better because I can usually finish my school-work for the day in two and a half hours if I keep at it. If we see ptarmigan out the window during school, my mom lets me take a break and go after them with my bow and arrow. If I get any, I take them to Aimo and Koonoo, an elderly Inuit couple here in town, because they really like to eat them.

When you're home-schooled, you don't have to be sitting at a desk to learn. You can bring school with you wherever you go, and you can learn from the land. For example, last fall my mom, my dad and I stayed for a month at a place called Bathurst Inlet on the Arctic coast. We were the only people there. Our job was to make sure that the grizzly bears didn't break into the houses. I brought my school books with me. When I was not doing school work, I was hiking around looking for caribou, wolverine, and grizzlies, checking the fish net, or hunting for seal.

In my free time, I like skidooing, kayaking, ice fishing, and summer fishing. I also like painting animals and other northern wildlife with acrylic paints; I sell my own art cards. I like whale-bone carving too.

When I shot my first caribou, we gave some meat to the elders. That's the tradition. I got my General Hunting Licence when I was ten years old, and I felt proud of that. It says I can legally hunt for caribou and certain other animals in the Northwest Territories and many other parts of Canada without needing a tag, although there are certain laws that must still be observed. It also means I can have a trapline and set a fish net.

I remember the first animal I ever shot, a grouse. I shot it with my .22 when I was five years old. I also snare rabbits. One time, a coyote took a rabbit from one of my snares. I went after the coyote on my snow machine and I caught it. Sometimes people take the animals like wolves, foxes, and wolverines to auction to sell the furs. I took my coyote to Koonoo, and she made me a pair of mitts from it.

When I was ten, I shot my first polar bear. We gave a lot of the meat to the elders in the community. I ate some—it tastes really good. It is an important event when an Inuk shoots his first polar bear. Everyone was congratulating me, even on the local radio station.

Learning about caribou hunting is important to me. I had harvested twenty-five caribou by the time I turned fourteen, but I am still learning. One of the things I am learning is that caribou migration routes sometimes change. One year we went to a place where we expected to find a herd, and we found no caribou at all. I later learned that the caribou had already migrated south of where we were. We went to a different camp that same fall, and found thousands of caribou.

Government scientists are doing caribou counts by helicopter in small areas of the Northwest Territories, and when they don't find them, they warn about the disappearance of the species. But I think the herd could have been over in Nunavut at the time of the caribou count in the Northwest Territories. I'm looking for more evidence.

I like seeing these animals and getting close to them. They are really beautiful, and sometimes you get to see thousands of them. Once my dad walked into the herd, and thousands of animals ran around him. Sometimes if you stand still, the caribou will approach you because they're curious. If you move, you will spook them. For me, being among the animals is the best part of hunting.

When we go hunting in the summer, we butcher the animal at the hunting site, then take it by motorboat back to our camp near the water. In winter, we also skin and butcher the animal wherever it falls, even if it is really cold out. Then we load everything, except maybe some of the guts, on a toboggan behind our snow machine.

On September 15, 2007, I harvested my first caribou with a bow and arrow. I was eleven years old. I have always been interested in hunting with a traditional recurve bow. This is different from the compound bows that most bow hunters use, which are more powerful and keep the arrow more still while they aim. Using a traditional bow is more challenging than hunting with a rifle or a compound bow because it's much harder to aim accurately. I have been hunting ptarmigan and ground squirrel with a bow since I was five.

Although I often brought my bow along on hunting trips and tried shooting at caribou a few times, in 2007 I decided that this was the year I was really going to do it. So that summer I did a lot of practising, shooting at a foam target to improve my aim. I pretty much taught myself how to shoot, although I did get some pointers from some of the sports hunters.

I was working with my family that September at a hunting camp at Thonokied Lake, near the Northwest Territories border with Nunavut. For several weeks, I went walking almost every day, looking for animals. Usually my mom followed me with the rifle for backup just in case we saw a grizzly bear. We walked and crawled in all kinds of weather—rain, snow, and wind. Sometimes I would shoot and miss, but I tried not to get discouraged.

Then one day while my mom and I were walking away from the camp, we saw four or five caribou. We kept walking, and then we saw a couple of hundred caribou in the distance, coming over a hill. We waited behind a rock for them to come by. A couple of caribou went right by me.

That's when I took aim. When they were less than three metres away, I pointed the arrow at the heart of a bull caribou. On the first try, he went down. I was surprised! I didn't think I would get one. We radioed my dad. He came and took pictures, and he was very proud of me. We brought the caribou back to the camp. We hung the meat up next to the camp, but that night a grizzly came and stole some of it.

I know that some people don't like the idea of killing animals. Some people are vegetarians. I met someone like that here in Yellowknife, and we talked about it. She thought that hunting was wrong. All I could say was, "That's the way we've lived for a really long time. This is the food we eat. This is the way we live."

I think I'll always want to live in the north, and I'll always want to go hunting on the land.

What do we know for sure ?

I talked to Devon Allooloo in his family home in Yellowknife and wrote down his words. He later checked this story and sent me his corrections. His family showed me many pictures of his hunting trips and explained different kinds of hunting to me.

It is possible that Devon is the youngest modern hunter on record to harvest a caribou with a traditional bow and arrow. The Pope and Young bow-hunting club in the United States—which keeps records for North America—wrote that Devon "is by far the youngest bow-hunter that we have heard of being successful in taking a caribou with a bow."

Young people of aboriginal ancestry are allowed to obtain a General Hunting Licence in the Northwest Territories at the age of ten for some important reasons.

Elders and parents want to train kids in hunting safety and traditions, the right way from the beginning. Northerners have been hunting caribou for thousands of years. For centuries the First Nations and the Inuit across the north relied on the caribou for survival. Devon's Inuit ancestors made warm clothing and tents from caribou skin. They made heat and light by burning caribou fat. They made sewing needles and scraping tools from the bones, and thread from the sinew. Caribou meat fed their big families and also fed the dogs that carried their belongings from place to place. All parts of the caribou were needed, and they were used carefully.

Today, caribou hunting remains an important way of life in the north—not to supply sewing needles or fuel like in the old days, but to feed families with delicious, healthy, affordable food. The caribou hunt is also an important part of Dene and Inuit storytelling and culture, and people don't want to lose it.

I talked to Devon about the caribou hunt at an interesting time. It seemed like every time we turned on the radio or TV in Yellowknife, we heard northerners talking about the future of the caribou herds.

Canada has more than 2.4 million caribou. They roam in huge herds through immense areas of forests, mountain valleys, and across the open tundra. There are four different kinds of caribou: the woodland caribou, the Peary caribou, the barren-ground caribou west of the Mackenzie River, and the barren-ground caribou east of the Mackenzie River.

The Canadian government says that the Peary caribou is an "endangered species" and the woodland caribou is a "threatened species," which means that we have to find ways to protect

Devon in traditional Inuit winter clothing inside *iglu*.

the animals from climate change, northern industry, and over-hunting if we want them to survive.

More than half the caribou in the north are barren-ground caribou—the kind that Devon hunts. So far they are not labelled "endangered" or "threatened" by the government. Government scientists are reporting a rapid decline in the herds, and they are concerned about it. Some other scientists, and many aboriginal northerners who are basing their estimates on the wisdom of their elders, are saying that the caribou migration patterns and calving areas change every few years, and that the government scientists may not have the most accurate information on numbers.

Fishing at Thonokied Lake, NWT.
COURTESY OF ALLOOLOO FAMILY COLLECTION

All northerners want to work together to protect the caribou herds, although they don't always agree on how to do it.

A few weeks before my conversation with Devon, the Northwest Territories government put a temporary ban on hunting the Bathurst caribou herd, north of Great Slave Lake to the Nunavut border. This is the area where Devon hunts. The Dene Nation—a group representing First Nations across the territory—says the government is interfering with treaty and aboriginal hunting rights and making a poor decision about the caribou too.

Devon is waiting to hear what the Northwest Territories Supreme Court will decide after listening to both sides. The young hunter is following this case with a lot of interest. He believes that Inuit and Dene hunters are conservationists and want to protect the caribou herds for future generations as much as environmental scientists do. In the meantime, the government is allowing aboriginal hunters who have a General Hunting Licence to hunt for buffalo. Devon has taken advantage of this opportunity: he harvested his first bison last December.

Aside from hunting and fishing, Devon, his two older sisters, and his parents have a special interest in keeping alive the Inuit tradition of *iglu* making. Devon also enjoys sports. When he was nine years old, he was practising his canoe safety skills one day with five other kids and two instructors in Back Bay. They heard cries for help. The kids and their leaders paddled out to a father and son in an overturned canoe, and pulled them to safety. They won an award for the rescue from the Lifesaving Society of Canada. Devon works with his family at NARWAL Adventure Training and Tours. After five years of home school, he is planning to go to high school in Yellowknife this fall.

Lexi Joinson of Old Crow, Yukon entered her
first dogsled race at the age of eight.

A Canadian Dog Musher
Goes to Russia

Lexi Joinson, age ten
Old Crow, Yukon, 2010

I love running sled dogs by myself. Everyone at my house likes dog mushing, and it all started with my dad. When he was younger, he used to run a whole bunch of sled dogs in Cumberland House, Saskatchewan. Then my mum got into it, and then my brother, sister, and I did too.

I am ten years old right now. I was born in Prince Albert, Saskatchewan, and I have already lived in Fort St. James, BC, and Dawson City, Yukon. We moved up to Old Crow last April. I had mixed feelings about moving. I didn't want to leave my friends behind, but I did want to explore and find out about new places. I like all the nice people up here, and we can just go anywhere in the bush. There are lots of great dogs in Old Crow too.

When I was a little kid, my family had a little batch of puppies. I stuck my head in the doghouse and I hardly ever came out. My family has plenty of dogs, but my own favourite is April. She is black and white with blue eyes, and she is very kind.

I started dogsledding by myself when I was eight. To help me get going, my dad took me out and showed me how to get the dog team ready, and how to ride the sled behind the dogs and guide them. After that, he took me out to a lake near our house. This big lake is almost one hundred kilometres long; in winter, it has thousands of trails going this way and that way around it. Dad told me to follow a certain loop in the trail that went over the snow for six kilometres. He explained everything I had to do. And then off I went—just the dogs and me!

My dad was a bit nervous as he watched me go. He waited. He waited some more. Maybe it seemed to him like I was gone forever. Was I lost? Was I in trouble? Finally I raced back to him on the dogsled with a big smile on my face. The dogs ran ahead of me, pulling me along the snow, and my dad could see that I was having fun.

Later I ran into our house, screeching with glee, to tell my Mum about it. I said I wanted two more dogs for our team, and she knew I was addicted to dogsledding forever.

I ran my first dogsled race against other people later the same year. I was still eight. There were three mushers in the race, and I was the youngest. The race was six kilometres long, and we ran two dogs with each sled. Another girl and I were side by side, and we were bumping our sleds, trying to get past each other. Every time I bumped into her, I said, "I'm sorry!" I wanted to be polite. I finished the race in seventeen minutes and came in second place.

■ ■ ■

One day last fall, I woke up in my bed to the sound of my mother's excited voice.

"Lexi! Come here right now!"

"What is it? I'm trying to sleep!"

"Just come!" Mum said.

I thought that I must be in trouble, because it sounded like something important, but I had no clue what I did wrong. I walked downstairs to find out what Mum was yelling about.

Waiting for her to tell me, I sat down on the last step.

Mum was sitting at the computer, reading her email. She looked up at me with a lot of happiness in her face. "We are going to a dogsled race in Russia!"

It turned out that Mum and Dad had been talking about this idea for a long time. At first, I was not too excited, because I was way too tired, but soon I started to look forward to our big trip. I had three long months to wait.

The night before we left Old Crow, I finished my packing. My teacher did not give me any homework, so I was very happy. Now all I had to do was clean my room, have a good sleep, and walk out the door.

"Remember, Lexi, you'll have work to do in Russia," Mum told me. "You won't be just a tourist. You'll be working with us as part of the team."

Mum must have told me a million times that this wasn't the kind of holiday where you lie around on a beach.

"It's an adventure," she said. "We are going to an orphanage for boys where they have a special program to teach the kids how to take care of sled dogs, and how to race them. The Nord Hope Race is for adults, but we'll need you to help take care of the dogs. Maybe you can encourage the kids at the orphanage too, and show them something about sled dog racing."

It sounded like a good job to me. Too bad I couldn't take my own dogs over to Russia. Dogs love adventures too. But travelling with dogs and equipment would cost too much money. Mum said the Canadian and American racers would run dogsleds with the Russians' malamutes, Siberian Huskies, and Alaskan Huskies. Our own dogs would wait for us at home.

No matter which way you travel, it is a long, long way from the small village of Old Crow, Yukon, to the small village of Vilakova in Russia.

Mum and I went to the Old Crow airport, and we flew down to Whitehorse, where we spent a couple of days. Then we flew to Vancouver, where we met my dad. The next day we flew to Seattle in the United States. A very tall, grey-haired man named Terry Hinesley met us there. He was going to be the Race Marshall for the Nord Hope Race in Russia. Terry has been a musher in the famous Iditarod race in Alaska, which is more than 1,850 kilometres long—and when he's not racing dogs, he's racing cars.

After we met Terry, the four of us jumped on a big plane to Paris, France, where we met most of the rest of our team: Joe, Leslie, and Caroline the vet. Caroline is also a veterinarian for the Iditarod race. Then we took another plane ride for three hours to get to Moscow, a big city that is the capital of Russia. Anya, our Russian interpreter, and Barbara, another musher, met us at the airport and showed us the way to Vilakova.

We travelled for eleven hours on a bus, so I was very tired when we finally reached the orphanage. We went into a long building that had six doors. Behind each door were two bunk beds. I picked a room and lay down on a bed. The pillows and mattresses were made of hay! Everything was so different from Canada.

"I have to be strong," I said to myself. "The opening ceremonies will begin in a few days."

■ ■ ■

My favourite part about Russia was the beautiful view of the countryside and the sweet people. Whenever I needed something, they would try hard to get it for me. The two cooks, Marina and Nina, always asked me, "Are you hungry?" Even though I said no, they would plop something humongous on my plate.

We lived with Russians in the orphanage. We ate meals with each other and learned how important food is to them. They eat a lot of salt because they believe it is a very important food. While we were there, they ate very little meat. The people we stayed with belong to the Russian Orthodox religion; it was Lent, so they didn't eat meat or milk for a little while before Easter. Also, they don't have as many animals to eat. They eat lots of homemade soup, with many good snacks.

Russia is an amazing place. Since we were staying at a Russian Orthodox orphanage, we went to see some of their oldest churches. Mother Paraskeva arranged a bus for us. Anton, our guide, was nineteen and training to be a priest. We are not part of the churches, but we listened to his prayer. We ladies had to wear a hat or scarf over our heads because it is not respectful to show your head.

Mother Superior gave me a crucifix because I like to learn about churches. Some Russian churches were built eight hundred years ago! Long ago, one church was abandoned when the people in charge decided to destroy all churches because the government was more powerful. That was the Soviet era, when Russia had a different kind of government.

Russian churches have amazing paintings and icons, which are beautiful pictures of saints on wood. One church was locked. We climbed up a staircase to see the bell tower. I saw a library halfway up the dark, twisted, stone stairway. Snow blew in, so we needed help getting up. All of the bells had been taken away. The Soviets had used the church for a storage room in the old days.

Mother Paraskeva runs the orphanage. She was very sweet and kind to me. She and I sat together a lot, and I would bring her tea. She would always drink all of it. Mother Paraskeva is the person who started the race and asked the boys of the orphanage to look after the dogs, so they have something to love and care for. During the Soviet times, she used to be a nuclear scientist.

I also met a Russian girl named Stacia, who was staying in the bedroom next to mine. She was nine years old and did not speak much English. Of course, I did not speak much Russian, either. Stacia knew how to say *yes* and *no* in English. For fun, we grabbed my washable markers and drew fake tattoos on each other and on ourselves. We also watched Tom and Jerry cartoons in Russian with English subtitles. Sometimes, we went outside and slid down a big ice hill and played with her dog, Stinker. (I think Stinker must mean something different in Russian!) Stacia and her dad gave me a Russian tuque, and I gave her some Canadian Olympic mitts. We lay on the ground, counted in our own languages, and then we copied each other. I started to learn Russian, and she started to learn English. We played the same games.

■　■　■

The opening ceremonies for the big race finally began on February 22. All around us, Russians started showing up by the hundreds.

Out of nowhere, someone grabbed my hand and pulled me into a dancing circle. Another dancer grabbed my hand and pulled me the other way. I felt like a tug-of-war toy. Finally, someone turned off the exciting Russian music, and the dancing stopped.

I looked up at the flags on the wooden poles and saw the

Russian flag going up. The Russian national anthem played on the big speakers. Everyone was watching. I realized that the Canadian flag was right next to the Russian flag. It made me feel welcome! The American flag was there too.

I ran into my bedroom and grabbed a bunch of red Canadian Olympic mittens and stuffed them down the front of my jacket. Outside, I started giving them away to the kids. At first they shook their heads and refused, because they thought they had to pay me. I ripped the price tags off, and then they nodded yes. Their faces brightened up. It was fun to look at their smiling faces when they had their mitts on their hands. They liked the Canadian stuff because it was from the Olympics.

With all the people gathering around the little farm, it looked like a small city for about two hours. I saw lots of Russian ladies wearing fur hats and jackets with fancy high-heeled boots. To me they did not look like they were dressed warmly enough for winter. Some didn't wear ski pants like Canadian women wear in the north at home. But many Russians wore boots called Vilinki, made out of dog hair and wool. In Russia they spin dog hair into warm material. We brought home lots of socks knitted from dog hair.

The race started at noon, right after the opening ceremony. It was a bright sunny day with only a few clouds in the sky. Even though I could see my own breath, I knew these dogs were going to sweat!

Dogs were barking as loudly as they could howl. They were jumping up and down and seemed excited for the race to begin. People crowded along the sidelines. Some people were petting and looking at the dogs. A Russian musher rode up with his team to the start line. Speaking in Russian, the officials counted down.

Пять *Five!*

Четыре *Four!*

Три *Three!*

Два *Two!*

Один *One!*

Поехали! *Go!*

With snow flying high in the air, the first musher and his team of six dogs rushed down the trail. The race was on!

Russian dogsledders teamed up with a Canadian or American musher to make an international team. Some of the Russian racers were kids from the orphanage. On the first day they ran the dogs for thirty-five kilometres, and then the American and Canadian partners ran fifty kilometres with their dogs the next day.

We watched two days of mushing, then we had a free day, and then we watched two more days of mushing. My mum and dad raced, and I cheered them on. Some of the racing dogs in Russia are big and shaggy. Alaskan Huskies have shorter hair and floppy ears. Malamutes and Siberian Huskies have longer hair but they don't have floppy ears. I love the Russian dogs because they are sweet and friendly.

My mom's racing dogs were named Boozer, Max, Vik, Vieter, and Beets. Mom had to drop Beets from the race because he had a sore knee. He was a shaggy white dog, and I hope he wasn't disappointed. Whenever dogs aren't feeling good, we make sure they take a break from racing. Dad had two dogs on his team named Silver and Booka, and he gave one dog the nickname Dumbo, because he had flapping ears just like the baby elephant in the movie.

Russia has a long winter just like Canada, but Russians don't have too many dogsled races in that area yet. On the free day,

Caroline, Leslie, and Barb explained different kinds of equipment to Russian mushers of all ages. They also talked about ways to take care of the animals.

I worked hard too. I helped some of the racers with their dogs and did some foot care, checking the dogs' paws for cracks and rub marks and applying ointment. And I helped my mom give her dogs water, because they wouldn't drink. We put a little milk in the water, and they drank a lot for me. Dogs need to be hydrated so they will be healthy and run better.

Pink ointment is a cream that is very stinky and sticky. You can put it on a dog's feet if they have a tender foot, or just before a race to get ready. It is even good for a human's skin. Mom's Russian racing partner, Cola, did not like the pink ointment to touch his hands, boots, or anywhere. Even though Cola doesn't like pink ointment, I think it feels really cool, and I helped smear it on some dogs' feet by myself.

Many Russian kids at the orphanage seemed interested when they saw me at work. Almost everybody loves dogs. We don't need to know English words or Russian words to explain these strong feelings. We understand each other.

What do we know for sure?

When I met Lexi Joinson in her classroom at Chief Zzeh Gittlit School in Old Crow, she mentioned that she would soon be travelling to Russia for a dogsled race. That sounded like a good story for this book. I asked her to send me an email about her adventures when she returned to Canada. Not only did she send me her story in mini-chapters in eight long emails, she also sent the pictures that you see here.

Visiting a Russian monastery with Anton and Jerry.
COURTESY OF JOINSON FAMILY COLLECTION

I put her stories together for this chapter, and then I called her back long-distance to ask for extra information. After reading my story, she added many extra sentences of her own and corrected my mistakes. I think she would be an excellent writer of her own books, don't you?

"Russia surprised me a lot," she told me. "It looked like nothing I expected." She would like to return to explore the whole country in the future.

Lexi loves travelling. "When I get older, I want to go to college and get a job and then explore the world," she said. Would you believe she's already raced dogs in Australia? As a prize at a dogsled race in the United States, the Joinson family won an all-expenses-paid trip to Australia. Despite the lack of snow in most places, many Australians are fans of the northern sport. Their dog teams pull riders on bike scooters instead of sleds, although there is a big hill in Australia with enough snow for one weekend-long dogsled race a year.

Back at home, Lexi prefers dogsledding for fun.

Traditionally, Inuit and First Nations people in northern Canada relied on dogs to help them carry their belongings from place to place. The dogs would carry packs on their backs, and the people would walk beside them on snowshoes. Later, northern Canadians of all backgrounds relied on dogsleds to take them long distances in the years before they had trucks, cars, or highways.

Today, skidoos, also called snowmobiles, have replaced dog teams for most transportation across deep snow. In isolated northern Canadian communities like Old Crow—which is a fly-in community without a highway—many families don't bother to buy a car or truck. Instead, they use a skidoo in the winter, and an all-terrain vehicle in the summer.

Dogsledding and dogsled racing remain popular sports in northern Canada, even if they are no longer needed as much for transportation. Lexi used the word "mushing" to talk about dogsledding. It comes from the command word used to tell dogs to go forward: "Mush!" Do you ever wonder about that odd word? When the early Canadian voyageurs ran their dog teams, they shouted: "Marche!" That's the word for "walk" in French. English-speaking dogsledders borrowed the word, and changed it a bit.

Mushers work hard to train the dogs for different jobs on the dog team. A leader dog goes first on the team, with point dogs, swing dogs, and wheel dogs running behind. All kinds of big, strong dogs can be seen on teams, but the most common breeds are malamutes, Alaskan Huskies, and Siberian Huskies.

Many northern kids enjoy another winter sport called skijoring. They put on cross-country skis, and then wear a hip harness with a bungee cord line attached to their dogs' harnesses. The kids push through the snow with ski poles, as the dogs race along the trail. Across the north, you will often see a family dog pulling a small child in a toboggan or sled for a quiet walk down the road.

Once in Old Crow, I saw a boy on a skidoo pulling another boy on a snowboard down a trail, and over high snowbanks. The snowboarder almost looked like he was surfing on waves of snow. They were having a lot of fun!

Dogsledding and skijoring are popular in many northern countries, including Russia. Mother Paraskeva and Father Bartholomew are former scientists who bought an old collective farm to start the St. Nicholas Russian Orthodox Parish and orphanage in rural Russia. They decided that the boys at the orphanage would benefit from the company of sled dogs. For the past few years, American dogsledder Terry Hinesly has taken a delegation of Canadian and American dogsledders to the Nord

Hope race at the orphanage. The village of Vilkova is about six hundred kilometres northeast of Moscow.

You can go to dogsled races all over northern Canada. One of the most famous races is the Yukon Quest, a sixteen hundred kilometre race from Fairbanks, Alaska, to Whitehorse, Yukon. See www.yukonquest.com for photographs, videos, and more information about dog teams.

In another story in this book, *The Iron Man of the Yukon Had Help*, on page 61, you can read why the Percy DeWolfe Memorial Mail Race began in Dawson City. Explore the website for the race at www.thepercy.com.

The Canadian Championship Dog Derby in Yellowknife, NWT, is one of the oldest sled dog races in North America.

Many Canadian dog mushers also compete in a famous American race called the Iditarod. Dogsleds travel more than 1,850 kilometres between Anchorage and Nome in Alaska in ten to seventeen days. See the video online at www.iditarod.com.

If you visit northern Canada yourself, you can go on your own dogsled tour across the snow to see the northern lights— just like Lexi.

Laurie and Tianna Reti and Suki.

Suki

Laurie Reti, age twelve, and Tianna Reti, age ten
Whitehorse, Yukon, 2010

Our family loves animals. We have nine kids in our family, including two twin sisters who are older than us, but we always have room in our house for pets and strays. Mum has let us keep rabbits, lizards, squirrels, fish, a bird who flew away at Christmas—and big dogs, medium dogs, and little dogs.

We met Suki in the summer of 2008. Our mum was working in a little café on Main Street called Baked, and we were helping out as gelato scoopers. (Gelato is something like ice cream, but softer and easier to scoop.) One day, Tony Zedda, the owner of the café, walked in the door with the tiniest, funniest dog we had ever seen in our lives. We fell in love with that puppy on the spot.

Dropping our gelato scoops in a hurry, we raced over to pat it on the head. Too bad, customers! In Whitehorse, dogs come first.

"What kind of dog is it?" we asked.

"She is part Pomeranian, part Butterfly," said Tony. "Her name is Suki. Would you like to hold her? She likes gentle people."

Suki fell in love with us on the spot. She could sit in the curve of our elbows with lots of room to spare. We took turns holding her and didn't want to see her go.

A few weeks later, Tony came to us with a problem. He had to leave Whitehorse for a few days, and he couldn't find anybody to take care of Suki.

"I can't leave this little dog with a stranger," he said. "She's too young and scared. Would you girls take care of her for me?"

Would we? Of course we would! We took her home and took

care of her for almost a week. We gave her a place to sleep in our house and good food to eat. We taught her tricks, like how to sit, how to beg, and how to roll over. She couldn't learn to roll over too well, but she kept trying.

Suki listened very well, and she was playful. She had pointed ears, shaped like butterflies. Her hair was soft, the colour of Yukon copper. She was so small she could fit inside a flowerpot, or the hood of a man's parka. Some grown-ups don't like yappy dogs like Suki, but we loved every yap.

Whitehorse is a place where dogs and kids have a lot of freedom. Together, kids and dogs can run out the back door of the house and race straight into the woods. Every day we took Suki on a leash for a walk on the hiking trails that criss-cross Whitehorse like green ribbons. You have to be careful, because many trails lead into a deep forest—the home of coyotes, foxes, squirrels, rabbits, lots of ravens and big birds, even bears far out of town. Dogs like to chase wild animals, and bark at them. If we didn't watch Suki, she might yap her way into big trouble.

We had another challenge with our little visitor too. You see, we have a dog of our own at home named Chico. Watching us play with Suki that week, Chico felt left out and lonely. Suki would bark at Chico, and that made everything worse. The tiny pup terrified our bigger dog with her yapping, and Chico would run away with hurt feelings and sore ears.

It was impossible for us to walk the two dogs on the trail at the same time. We couldn't walk together, so we stayed apart. That seemed to work. In Whitehorse you meet lots of dogs on the hiking trails, and on the streets, walking their humans. Sometimes Chico took us for walks by herself. That made her feel better.

One day we were walking with Chico on the sidewalk near our house, when a yellow taxi went by us. We watched as the taxi stopped in the middle of the street, and backed up slowly. The driver pulled over and shouted to us.

"*Bonjour!* Hello! *Comment ca va?* How are you?"

We knew it must be Robert Roux. He knows our family. He's a famous Whitehorse taxi driver who likes to speak in two languages at once.

"Cute little *chien* you've got there, *mes amis*," he said. "Do you mind if I take a photograph?

He pointed his camera at Chico and us. All three of us smiled at the same time. We didn't know it then, but he took the photograph and created a beautiful painting on his computer. He came into Picka Peppa—that's our mum's restaurant—and gave a copy of his artwork to our mum.

We get to meet all of the interesting people of Whitehorse because of our restaurant. People outside the Yukon don't know much about our city, and maybe they think we all live in igloos, and that we're always freezing cold in the snow all year round. That is not true!

On warm summer days, kids in Whitehorse like to ride bikes on the trails, with dogs running beside them. One time our mum took us to see a friend, Ian, at Sky High ranch. He must have about a thousand dogs up there for dogsledding in the winter, and he has horseback riding in the summer. We loved watching some dogs jumping through hoops. On another summer day, we baked some cookies and put them outside to cool. Through the window, we saw a Whitehorse dog munching every cookie!

Are you wondering what happened to tiny Suki? Well, at the end of his week away, Tony came back and picked her up. We were sad to see her go, but we visited her a lot. Then one day Tony told us he would have to find a new home for Suki because his wife was having a baby—and a newborn baby and a yappy puppy can be a bit too noisy if they live in the same house.

Tony found a family that wanted Suki for a pet. We understood. We already had Chico as our family dog, so we said goodbye.

We miss Suki all the time. She was unusual because most northern dogs are much bigger. Wherever we go in Whitehorse, we keep our eyes open for a tiny dog with butterfly ears, and we keep our ears open for the yappiest yap in the Yukon. That would be our friend Suki—a Yukon dog that will never pull a dogsled!

What do we know for sure?

I bet you can figure out how I met Laurie and Tianna Reti.

One lucky day in Whitehorse, I took a Yellow taxi to the Yukon Archives, and spoke in French and English to a taxi driver named Robert Roux. We started to talk about his good friend and customer, Jim Robb, who is a wonderful Yukon storyteller and artist. The taxi driver pulled his picture of Jim out of his file folder on the front seat. I asked if I could look at his other artwork. When I found the painting of Laurie and Tianna and the tiny dog, I asked for the story behind the picture.

Robert told me to go to the Picka Peppa restaurant, *toute de suite!*

A few weeks later, I found the girls' mum, Andrea, cooking in the kitchen at Picka Peppa. She is known as one of the best cooks in Whitehorse, and her specialty is jerk chicken and sweet potato pie. Born in Jamaica, Andrea came to Canada in 1990. She lived in Ontario for ten years, before moving west to Vancouver, Whitehorse, Old Crow, and back to Whitehorse again. She asked me to come back to the restaurant the next day so that Laurie and Tianna could tell me Suki's story.

The girls love their hometown. After they told me about the tiny dog, they described what kids like to do in Whitehorse, the capital of Yukon Territory.

"Whitehorse is a refreshing place, not that polluted at all, and quiet," said Tianna, whose full name is Tatiana. "You can do a lot of skiing, snowboarding, skating, and sledding here." Mountains and forests surround the small city, and the Yukon River flows right through the middle of town.

"Our favourite sledding places are the Big V, a big, snowy place where two hills connect, or Mount Sima," said Laurie. "Every winter we have the Yukon Sourdough Rendezvous, a big winter festival, with races, ice castles, dancing, and *cabane à sucre*." That's a French way of saying sugar shack. A big Canadian tradition is to take the sap from the trees in the spring, and heat it until it becomes delicious homemade syrup for pancakes.

The Reti sisters are students at Selkirk Elementary School in Whitehorse. Laurie likes dancing—hip-hop, jazz, and ballet—and she plays basketball, performs in talent shows, and acts in plays such as *How the Grinch Stole Christmas*. Tianna likes to play soccer and basketball and sing in musicals. Both girls enjoy reading books and watching movies about dogs, and they like to swim and skate at the Canada Games Centre.

Their best friends, Kate and Mary, are also sisters. In the summer, the four girls like to search for flowers on hikes around the town. They find crocuses, daisies, sunflowers, and wildflowers. Walking through the woods behind their house, Laurie and Tianna follow hiking trails to interesting ponds. One summer day they caught forty-five frogs in one pond, and seven more frogs in another pond. They took them home, and kept them overnight, but returned them to the ponds the next day. (Their mum was relieved to see the frogs go home.)

They asked that I please include in this chapter all the names of their brothers and sisters, so here they are in order: Troy, Nicole, Daniel, Jordan, Phillip, Anya, and Shanice.

For Tianna and Laurie, dogs aren't just best friends, they're family members. Aside from Suki the visitor, and Chico, family dogs have included Rezz and Nanook.

Whitehorse has been called the best city for dogs in Canada. In 2009 a writer named Katherine Sandiford investigated this happy situation in a story for *Up Here*, a great magazine about northern Canada. "With an average of one dog per household, and plenty of room to romp leash-free," she wrote, "Whitehorse may well be the world's mecca for mutts."

How many cities in the world allow dogs to swim in a million-dollar public swimming pool complex? That's what happens in Whitehorse. One day a year—on the day before the pool cleaning—the wading pool is closed to humans and open only to the city's dogs. They can yelp, splash, bark, dog paddle, and dive as much as they like. Katherine saw one pup in a lifejacket and doggles—a water mask for dogs.

Whitehorse is one of the few places where peaceful dogs are

allowed on ski trails, inside some stores and business offices, even inside the Whitehorse United Church for a special Blessing of the Animals service every year.

Why is the city so friendly to dogs? Katherine suggests in her story that it has to do with Yukon history and tradition. In the past, the First Nations relied on their dogs to help them carry their family belongings in side packs. Later, dogsledding became an important form of transportation for everybody in the years before cars, trucks, and roads came to the Yukon—and then it became a popular winter sport.

Call of the Wild is one of the most famous books ever written about the Yukon. In the story, writer Jack London describes the adventures of a dog named Buck during the Klondike gold rush. Today, Yukon Territory loves dogs so much that it is has a dog on its flag.

Pomeranians are one of the world's smallest dog breeds. You might not believe it, but some of Suki's ancestors in northern Europe were working dogs that pulled dogsleds too! Hundreds of years ago, the breed was much, much bigger and stronger. Later, they were bred to be small household pets and became very popular after Queen Victoria fell in love—on the spot—with a Pomeranian.

Laurie and Tianna don't know exactly where Suki lives today, but they will find her. Meanwhile, they invite all dogs and their humans to move to Whitehorse.

Aramayis Mikayelyan of Yellowknife.

Phone Call to Armenia

Aramayis Mikayelyan, age eight
Yellowknife, Northwest Territories, 2010

—Are you there, Arman?

—Yes, of course, I'm here. I've been waiting for the phone to ring. What did you do today, Aramayis?

—A writer came to my house to ask me about my life! She's writing my story in a book about kids in northern Canada. I kept talking and talking to her, and she wrote everything down in her notebook.

—You're going to be in a book? Did I hear that right?

—Yes, you did hear right. I told her about you. So you'll be in this book too.

—What did you tell her about me? Tell me right now. I hope you told her that I was your best-looking and smartest cousin!

—Are you joking? I told her you that were seven years old, and you live far away in Armenia with my other cousins. I told her that we like to talk on the phone.

—That's true. Did you tell her you sent me a PlayStation3, and that I like it?

—Of course I did. We had everything ready for her when she knocked on the door. Tatik had baked *gata* for her, and we gave her some Armenian *surtch* that she liked very much. She kept eating treats and drinking coffee while she asked me questions.

—With her mouth full?

—Yes!

—That must have looked funny! Did you show her my picture?

—Of course I did. She asked me where I would take you if you ever came to visit me in Yellowknife.

—Tell me!

—If you came in summer, Arman, I would take you outside to find a snack right away. We'd get a bit of money from my dad. Maybe we'd go with my friend Coulton—he's a good person—and buy slushies, beef jerky, and Doritos. Then we would take turns on my bike. We would ride to the soccer field, or play other games out in the field with my friends Ethan and Noah and Logan and Matthew.

—But how would I understand your Canadian friends? I can't speak English like you.

—Arman, nobody needs to speak English to play soccer in Yellowknife. You just kick the ball and run. My friend in school speaks another language because he just came here from the Philippines. He plays with us too. After the game we would take you to the beach.

—You have beaches in that cold country? Isn't it cold all the time?

—No, we have hot summer days and a big blue lake almost as big as an ocean. It's called Great Slave Lake, and it's my favourite place in the summer. You can see people in canoes, kayaks, sailboats, houseboats, and motorboats. Small planes zoom in from the sky and land on the water. In summer, all the Armenians in Yellowknife get together for a big picnic beside the lake. If you came with us, I would put bug spray all over you so the giant mosquitoes couldn't chew you up to little pieces.

—Giant *what*?

—Don't worry. Giant mosquitoes and blackflies only eat your ears and ankles and the back of your neck. If you come to Yellowknife in the summer, we could also go camping and listen to the wolves howl at the moon.

—WOLVES? Did you say wolves live near Yellowknife? Do they have big teeth? Could they swallow two cousins in one gulp?

—Don't worry so much, Arman! The wolf is my favourite animal. I've seen two of them already. They don't come into town. They live way, way out in the bush. I saw wolves from our car when we were driving on our holiday. I like the silver wolf best. Most Canadian wolves are afraid of people and stay away from us, but when we were driving down to Alberta, we did see a bear family . . .

—BEARS! Did they climb into your car to attack you? Did they chase you down the road?

—No, they ran into the bush as soon as they saw us. And don't worry. If you came here in the winter, they would be sleeping.

—Good! I won't wake them up! What would we do if I visited you in the winter?

—Well, on a cold, cold, cold, cold, cold day, we could stay inside and play my Wii and video games. On a regular cold, cold day, we would pull on our winter clothes and go out and play in the snow.

—What do you wear outside in January in Yellowknife?

—In winter in Canada, you have to pull on lots of clothes.

First you pull on your long johns and heavy socks.

Then you pull on jeans and a shirt.

Then you pull on heavy snow pants and a big coat with a zipper.

After that you pull on a neck-warmer.

Then you pull on a wool hat.

Next you pull your hood over everything else on your head, and you pull a scarf up around your face, and tie it in a knot at the back of your hood.

Then you pull on high, warm snow boots. At the very end, you pull on two pairs of mitts . . . and then you're warm.

—How could I walk if I'm wearing all that stuff? Do Canadians walk like robots through the snow?

—I walk like any normal kid in Armenia—only I'm dressed like a Canadian. When we walk down the street, we can hear the clean snow squeak under our boots.

—So what would we do next?

—I would take you all to all the high hills around Yellowknife. We could throw snowballs, or go tobogganing, or build a snow fort under the trees. When I was in Grade 2, our class went to a place where we could ride on dogsleds and skidoos over the snow. I liked riding with the dogs way better. It was fun. And sometimes we go to a special camp to learn about living on the land. The lady gives us bread called bannock and dry caribou meat that tastes just like *basturma* in Armenia. We could warm our hands near the campfire and drink hot chocolate.

—What would we do after that?

—To warm up, I would take you to the museum to play in the wall tent and tipi. Last Sunday I was coming out of the door of the museum with my parents and I saw a lynx in the snow—just behind the trees. A lynx is like a lion.

—A LION? You have lions in Canada too? Did it growl at you? Did it chase you around the museum until you screamed for help?

—I'm teasing you again. A lynx is more like a small wildcat, and they don't come into Yellowknife too often. They have soft fur and pointed ears. The one I saw near the museum must have been lost, but we do see lots of ptarmigan in town.

—Ptarmi-what? Are they wild beasts too? Do they eat people? Are they dangerous?

—Ptarmigan are peaceful birds that hide in the snow. They like to live in cold, fun places like Yellowknife.

—Just like you, Aramayis?

—Just like me.

What do we know for sure?

When Aramayis Mikayelyan told me how much he likes to talk on the phone with his cousin, Arman Armenakyan, I made up this story about their funny telephone conversation to make them both laugh. Aramayis read the story with his parents, and he liked it. He said I could put it in the book.

Aramayis is now nine years old. I had the good luck to meet him at the Prince of Wales Northern Heritage Centre in Yellowknife on the Sunday he spotted the lynx just outside the museum. We started to talk, and he and his parents, Hmayak and Satenik, invited me to their cosy apartment for Armenian treats a few nights later.

That's when Aramayis told me the story of his life.

He was born in Nor Hajn, Armenia, on June 22, 2001. Armenia is a beautiful country in central Asia. The town of Nor Hajn is famous around the world for the expert diamond polishers who live there—and Aramayis's father used to be one of them.

Sparkling diamonds in the Northwest Territories brought the family to Canada. Not long ago, about thirty-five diamond polishers from Nor Hajn travelled to Yellowknife to work in Canada's diamond industry. When he was three years old, Aramayis moved with his parents to join his grandparents and his uncle in Yellowknife. Counting the children, the Armenian community in Yellowknife adds up to about one hundred people.

On the weekends, the kids learn how to write in Armenian from a friendly teacher, and the families celebrate Armenian holidays together. The newcomers gave a big cross to St. Patrick's Catholic Church in the city, and some of them married local people. One woman started an Armenian cooking class for other Yellowknifers. A talented musician, Aramayis's father performs Armenian folk music around the city to make people happy.

The Northwest Territories is one of the largest diamond producers in the world. Every diamond needs a polisher. Sadly, the diamond polishing business has had its troubles in northern Canada. The Arslanian Cutting Works recently went out of business, and Aramayis's father lost his job, along with the other workers, most of them from Armenia. This problem has brought a lot of worry, and everybody hopes the factory will open again soon. Aramayis's parents found other jobs in Yellowknife, so the family is doing okay. It takes courage to move to a new country. Fortunately, the Mikayelyan family has lots of courage.

Aramayis is a student at Ecole St. Joseph School, where kids can study in English or French. After school, he loves to make crafts, watch television, and read books about northern animals, although his favourite book so far is *The Diary of a Wimpy Kid*. He has a younger brother named Mikayel.

Aramayis loves the wild animals of the north. "My favourite animal really is the wolf," he says. "Some are grey, black, white, and red. I have also seen bears and buffalo when we're driving on holidays."

Aramayis learning about traditional Dene food on a school field trip.

He speaks fluent English and Armenian and he can read a bit of Russian too. When he calls his cousin Arman on the phone, they always speak Armenian. The two boys met when they were very little, but they don't remember their visit. Their long-distance chats on the phone bring them together.

People in the Northwest Territories speak many languages. The territory is the ancestral home of the Dene, the Inuit, and the Metis people, and it has welcomed every other kind of Canadian too. More than half the forty-two thousand people in the territory have aboriginal ancestry. The territory has eleven official languages: English, French, Cree, Tłı̨chǫ, Chipewyan, South Slavey, North Slavey, Gwich'in, Inuvialuktun, Inuktitut, and Inuinnaqtun. That's more official languages than any other province or territory in Canada.

About twenty thousand people live in Yellowknife, the capital of the Northwest Territories. Walking through town, you're likely to hear languages from all over the world. About five hundred newcomers have arrived in the city from other countries in the past decade—from Africa, Asia, the Middle East, Central and South America, and Europe. Thousands of international tourists also come here every year to explore the northern wilderness and catch a glimpse of the mysterious northern lights. For more pictures and information about Aramayis's home territory, see www. spectacularnwt.com.

If you know any kids who are looking for a good hometown, tell them to move to Yellowknife. Aramayis says the wild animals aren't one bit scary.

Fourteen of the Greatest Kids in the World

The Grade 4, 5, 6 Class
Chief Zzeh Gittlit School
Old Crow, Yukon, 2010

Once upon a winter in Old Crow, we walked into our unusual classroom to begin an unusual day.

Why is our classroom unusual? If you came here, you would see the usual students' desks, teacher's desk, whiteboard, maps, bookshelves, and computer corner. But inside our classroom, we also have a northern cabin with real caribou antlers over the front door.

Whenever we want to read, and our work is finished, we can leave our desks and go inside the cabin with a book. We can sit on comfortable benches and whisper to each other, or climb a ladder to a loft for a little quiet time on our own.

Anyway, on this unusual morning in February, we walked past the cabin, sat down at our desks, looked up and saw a stranger. Who was she, anyway?

"This is a writer from Edmonton," our teacher, Ms. Cretney, explained. "She's travelling from place to place in northern Canada to talk to kids, and find out their true stories for a book. Do you have a story you'd like to tell her?"

Hmm. Maybe yes, maybe no.

The stranger asked us to write down our favourite things— just to warm up our imaginations for a little storytelling later.

So we started writing.

Cheyanne, who sometimes spells her name ShyAnn, wrote

that she loves the colour blue, ice cream, going to the mountains, and listening to music by Rhianna and Lady Gaga.

Melayna wrote that she likes rabbits, banana popsicles, floor hockey, and playing Guitar Hero. Her favourite place in Old Crow is the baseball field.

Madison wrote that she enjoys basketball and soccer, spaghetti, kittens and hamsters, horses and puppies, and scary stories.

Janelle wrote that she loves the colour red, hockey, cotton candy, and vampire stories, especially the book *New Moon* in the Twilight Saga. Her favourite animal is a wolf and her favourite meal is caribou heart.

Willow's favourite place in Old Crow is a special hill beside her own house. She likes to play Wii and Nintendo, and she likes to read books in the *Bone* series and the *Goosebumps* series.

Ty likes ice hockey, wolves, eagles, comic books, and funny people. His favourite place in Old Crow is his own house. His favourite colour is green, and his favourite music is AC/DC and rap music.

Lexi loves dogs, dogsledding, music, travelling, and meeting new people.

Nathanial loves the skateboard park in Old Crow, wolves and cougars, orange popsicles, Xbox video games, and eating caribou meat.

Like most kids in Old Crow, Aaron, Christopher, and Caleb like outdoor winter sports like skidooing and hockey at the arena, going to the Old Crow Youth Centre after school, and playing video games.

Then the stranger asked us to write our own stories, anything true that came to mind. We started to write them in class. Some of us finished them at home and brought them to school the next day and gave them to her.

Dakota wrote an interesting tale called "Going For Wood," about filling up his Bravo skidoo with gas so he could find more firewood for his family's camp. He drew pictures of big skidoos, tents, and firewood to illustrate his story.

Percilla loves her family very, very much, so she filled her life story with the names of her parents, her four grandparents, seven sisters, seven uncles, seven aunties, and twenty-three cousins. This story filled three pages with a lot of love.

Shaylene wrote about a few days in her own busy and interesting life. Would you like to hear it? Well, here it is.

Me and My Friends: A True Story
by Shaylene

One day me and my friends went sliding. I almost fell off of the cliff, but my friend grabbed my arm, and I said thank you.

Then we went back to Percilla's house and warmed up. When we finished warming up, we went back to the hill on the Bravo. (A kind of skidoo.) I saw my brothers Aaron and Cameron, and they threw snowballs at us.

We went down, and drove back up. Me and Percilla hit our knees on rocks. I said "Ow, ow, ow! Ooo, that hurts!" Percilla laughed, but I was okay with her laughing at me.

I went home and ate caribou meat and rice. It was delicious. My brother Aaron wanted me to write about us, oldest to youngest. I'll start, I said. Darcy, me, Aaron, Cameron. Then he said, "That's right!"

"Well, bye," I said. Then I said, "Dad, can I camp with Percilla tonight because it's Friday?"

Me and Percilla sneaked for a snack. It was funny. I hit my head under the table. "I think they heard us," I said. I got scared, but it was kind of funny.

"We should ask Melayna to camp too," I said. Percilla said okay. I said, "Let's phone her."

Melayna asked at home, and she was allowed, but me and Percilla had to meet her half way on the trail. She took longer than a minute, but she finally came. Me and Percilla said, "You took a long time." We finished our talk and went back to Percilla's house. I was really tired so I fell asleep until the next day.

It was foggy. I went home, and then went to the store with ten dollars in cash. I got a pop, chips, and a popsicle. We all walked up with them. It was kind of boring that day. But I went to make a snowman, and that was fun. I put rocks for eyes, and a stick for a nose. When I went to check on my snowman later, there was dog pee on it. Then I covered that part with snow and told Percilla and Melayna. They thought it was funny . . .

Then I went home, ate, and then made a fort outside. It took about one day to make. I went to bed for school the next day.

Then me and Percilla were buddy reading. I read to her. At hot lunch me and my friends sat together and after school Melayna and Percilla and me went to the College. I did MSN. I added Percilla and Melayna and Willow, Camisha, April, Jocelyn, Aaron, and Darcy. I had more friends to add but I couldn't find their email addresses. So I asked my friend. She didn't know.

It was time to go. I went to the store, played at Percilla's grandma's house, then I went home. I went to bed at 9:00 PM at night. I was really tired. I got up at 7:40, got dressed, washed my face, and then I ate. Then I went to school for a snack. I had an apple. It was juicy. Then I had a yogurt. It was blueberry. Then we did spelling and reading, and then it was time for hot lunch. We had Jell-O with Cool Whip on it and then me and Percilla, we had Cool Whip on our noses. Janelle tasted it. She said, "Mmm! That was good! I should get some!" That was funny. We really laughed hard.

Shaylene's story might have continued for a few more pages if she'd had just a bit more paper. She is a very busy person!

The next day, Ms. Cretney said it was okay for a few of us to sit at the round table at the back of the classroom to tell the writer about our adventures.

A bunch of us crowded around the table and talked quickly. The writer scribbled our words in her notebook as fast as she could.

First, she asked us if we like to go to culture camp.

Of course we do! We told her we go to the camp every spring to learn about life on the land. It is a part of school—only all out in the bush. We don't worry about the snow on the ground, because we can sleep in warm canvas tents and eat good food beside a wood stove or a campfire. We learn how to be good hunters and trappers, how to set snares, how to dry fish and caribou meat. Our teachers on the land last year were Florence Netro and Stanley Njootli, and other people too.

We don't just work all the time at culture camp. We play games and have fun. We tell a lot of jokes to each other. We stay on the land for days and days. Our families can come and visit us in the evenings. At night, older people tell us Van Tat Gwich'in stories from long ago. We can't wait to go back to the culture camp this year in March or April.

The writer closed her notebook, thanked us, and said good-bye. She promised to send our story back to us so we could check it before she put it in the book.

So that's what happened on an unusual day in our unusual classroom—and that's the end of our unusual story.

We all plan to live happily ever after.

What do we know for sure?

I visited Chief Zzeh Gittlit School on three different days when I was in Old Crow, and I think it's one of the most beautiful schools in the north.

The school has a gigantic playground, a huge gym where the community can gather for feasts, and extra-big classrooms. Kids can also sit and relax in a cosy place in the front hall under pictures of the Van Tat Gwich'in elders of Old Crow.

When I was sitting in this comfortable place, waiting for class to begin, a young girl named Maddy sat down and told me her story about a baby moose named Billy Bob who went to see a doctor and pretended he had a broken leg. It was quite a funny story, but it ended quickly because Maddy had to eat her lunch.

Young adults who are studying how to be chefs at Yukon College come to the school during the week to create delicious hot lunches for the kids. Sometimes they make caribou burgers, even caribou pizza! Once a month, students with perfect attendance get to take home a huge free pizza for their families.

If you go to the school's website, you can see cool pictures of the students on a caribou hunt, and on a muskrat trapping trip to Crow Flats. The link is www.yesnet.yk.ca/schools/chiefzzehgittlit/.

You'll find lots more pictures at the Old Crow community website: www.oldcrow.ca.

One of the teachers at Chief Zzeh Gittlit School built the reading cabin for the Grades 4, 5, 6 class, right inside their classroom. They really like it. Every afternoon the kids go to a different classroom to study the Gwich'in language with their teacher, Jane Montgomery, and do special projects. Jane gave me a dictionary so I could put some Gwich'in words in this book. I've been trying to teach myself to say them, and to remember a few words like these:

gwandak ~ story
màhsi' ~ thank you
ch'ii ~ mosquito
tsaiidhòh that datl'òo ~ blue jeans
zhoh ~ snow
shih ~ grizzly bear

I even learned how to say something kind of funny in Gwich'in: *Dzìh dahk'wàn kwaa!* That means "Quit cracking your gum!"

After I spoke to the kids in the combined Grade 4, 5, 6 class, I went to talk to Florence Netro in her office across the hallway. At the time of my visit, she was the Education Support Worker who organized the culture camp for the students and teachers. She showed me many pictures on her computer of the kids enjoying themselves at the camp.

"We take the whole school out on the land," she said. "It is an important part of their school year."

At camp the students learn practical skills, such as how to set rabbit snares, and how to skin a muskrat. They sleep in canvas tents, lit with small lamps, but they also learn how make emergency sleeping shelters out of spruce boughs and snow.

Students practise snowshoeing and cross-country skiing. They go on dogsled rides, and they learn how to take good care of dogs. The older kids go on a skidoo trip on trails that have been known to the Van Tat Gwich'in for thousands of years.

Around the campfire they learn how to prepare cranberry jam and Labrador tea and lots of delicious recipes with caribou meat. Sometimes they learn a little bit about sewing and traditional beading.

In the evenings, elders and other adults at the camp tell traditional Van Tat Gwich'in stories. These stories are told again and again, year after year, so nobody will ever forget them. They have been passed down to kids for generations.

Some traditional stories explain the clan system of families, and tell how the Crow clan, Deetrù, and the Wolf clan, Ch'ichyàa, came to be. Some magical stories are about heroes with special powers, like the story about "The Boy in the Moon." Some are scary stories about the *nanaa'in*, or the wild bushmen who hide in the woods and cause big trouble for people. Some are animal stories like "Ts'alvit, Deetrù'hah," which means the Loon and the Crow in Gwich'in. Many stories are about the history of the Gwich'in people.

You can read these stories for yourself in a new book that the community created together in ten years of hard work. The book is called *People of the Lake: Stories of Our Van Tat Gwich'in Elders.*

Florence Netro loves these stories. She grew up on the land with her family. Sadly, her father and two brothers died of whooping cough when she was very young. Her mother, Mary Netro, raised her six daughters—Helen, Dorothy, Kathy, Florence, Lorraine, and Sarah—by herself.

"My mum was our teacher. She taught us hunting and trapping. In the spring, we would go muskratting for three months . . . It was the happiest time that I can remember. I'm happy now because my mum taught us how to be positive, and how to work towards that. She told me, 'If you're negative, you're going to be sick inside. Be positive for your own health.'"

Mary Netro sewed warm fur parkas, mukluks, and warm mitts out of caribou hide to keep her six daughters warm outside in the winter. She taught the girls how to fish and hunt for caribou. Out on the land on Crow Flats, they camped in canvas tents. In the summer, they picked cranberries, blueberries, and salmonberries. Mary loved travelling across the land, right up until the time she died at the age of eighty-eight. Her big family still likes to go to her trapline across the Porcupine River.

"My parents taught us years ago to trust and be honest with one another in order to survive in this north," Florence told me. "All of the old traditions are not practised now, but they will be again. If we work on it in this next generation, it will continue to happen."

I love those words . . . and so I will end this book with them.

Acknowledgments

Storytellers of all ages worked with me to adapt their life stories for this book. Their family members searched for pictures and extra details, and went out of their way to help me. Thank you, friends. I will never forget the warmth of your welcome.

I am also grateful to the generous people of Dawson City, Yukon, where I made my home as Writer in Residence at Berton House in the winter of 2009. The Writers' Trust of Canada supports this wonderful residency—and I appreciated the help of James Davies in Toronto and the Dawson City Library Board as hosts.

I relied on the expertise of many traditional knowledge specialists for northern First Nations, especially Georgette McLeod, Angie Joseph-Rear, Sue Parsons, and Glenda Bolt of the Tr'ondek Hwëch'in; and Megan Williams, Mary Jane Moses, and Jane Montgomery of the Van Tat Gwich'in. I would also like to thank Gayle Corry of the Council of Yukon First Nations and Michelle Kolla of the Skookum Jim Friendship Centre. I am grateful to the Attawapiskat First Nation council, staff, and citizens for their help during my visit.

Along with storytellers at kitchen tables, and oral history experts, archivists and librarians are my best friends. I would like to thank Susan Twist, Donna Darbyshire, Shannon Olson, and Janelle Hardy of the Yukon Archives in Whitehorse; Laura Mann and Molly MacDonald at Dawson City Museum; everyone at the Dawson City Community Library; Mairi Macrae at the Whitehorse Public Library; Brenda Hans and Susan Irving of the Prince of Wales Northern Heritage Centre in Yellowknife; Ramona Rose and Erica Hernandez of the Northern BC Archives; Patricia

Kother of the Atlin Historical Society of Atlin, BC; as well as the special collections staff at the Alaska State Library in Juneau and the University of Washington in Seattle. Their help was invaluable.

Photographer Kayley Mackay of Yellowknife contributed creative energy and many photographs to this project. I was also fortunate to collaborate with cinematographer Peter Dreimanis and photographer Liam Sharp in Attawapiskat. I would like to thank Michele Royle of the Yukon Department of Education for thoughtful assistance, and principal Steve Climie of Chief Zzeh Gittlit School in Old Crow and teacher Peter Menzies of Robert Service School in Dawson City for welcoming me into classrooms. I'm also grateful to teacher Clair Dragoman for his beautiful photographs, and to Betty and Dan Davidson for guiding me to him.

I have appreciated the generous support of the Canada Council and the Alberta Foundation for the Arts and their joint program, the Alberta Creative Development Initiative. I am also deeply grateful to the Edmonton Arts Council for supporting my work, and for its stellar advocacy for the arts in my hometown.

Ruth Linka of Brindle & Glass Publishing has been a constant friend and supporter of my book projects since 2002. No writer could ask for a finer publisher. I am also grateful to an inspired editor, Lynne Van Luven in Victoria; to copy editor Christine Savage; and to other staff members at Brindle & Glass, Emily Shorthouse, Tara Saracuse, and designer Pete Kohut.

Kira Dreimanis and Anne Cameron-Sadava offered personal encouragement throughout this long project, and I will remember it. Finally I would like to thank my husband, Allan Chambers, for his belief in my work, and for his patience. More than anyone, he understands how much every story matters to me.

About the Author

Linda Goyette is a writer, editor, and journalist with a strong interest in oral history and contemporary storytelling in Canada. She is the author of two other story collections for young readers, *Rocky Mountain Kids* and *Kidmonton*. Her previous books for adults include *Edmonton In Our Words, Standing Together, The Story That Brought Me Here,* and *Second Opinion.* She lives in Edmonton with her husband, Allan Chambers, and their two dogs, Franny and Zooey. To reach her, visit www.lindagoyette.ca